The Church in Communist China

FRANCIS PRICE JONES

THE CHURCH IN

COMMUNIST CHINA

A Protestant Appraisal

FRIENDSHIP PRESS   NEW YORK

Library of Congress Catalog Card Number: 62-7859

*Dedicated to the friends and colleagues
of former days who are still bearing witness
to the Christian gospel in Communist China*

GUIDE TO PRONUNCIATION

The standard Wade system of transliteration of Chinese characters has been used for most of the proper names in this book. In this system the letters have for the most part their values as in common English usage. The following notations cover the chief variations.

VOWELS:

> *a* regularly broad, as in *ah*
> *ao* rhymes with *cow*
> *e* regularly short
> *i* as in *machine;* if followed by *n* or *ng* short as in *pin;* also short in *ih*
> *ie or ieh* approximately equivalent to English *yea*
> *o* long, but not closing with an *u* sound
> *ou* long *o,* closing with *u*
> *u* as in English; before *ng* more like long *o*

CONSONANTS:

The consonants *p, t, k, ch* and *ts,* when followed by an apostrophe, have approximately their English sound. Without the apostrophe they are roughly equivalent to *b, d, g, dj* and *dz* respectively. Thus the newspaper *Ta Kung Pao* (see chapter 4) is pronounced Dah Goang Bow. Sometimes the apostrophe is omitted where it logically should be found; thus the church magazine *Tien Feng* is pronounced with a *t* and not a *d* sound. *k* before *i* has the sound of *ch (dj)*; thus Kiang Wen-han's surname has the same sound as Chiang Kai-shek's. We use the spellings as preferred by the persons themselves.

J represents a peculiar sound which is really closer to the English *r*; Jao Shu-shih (chapter 3) has a surname roughly equivalent to the first syllable of *rowdy*. *Hs* appears only before *i* or umlaut *u*; it is about the same as *sh*, only pronounced a little farther forward in the mouth.

The spelling of a few names deliberately disregards this Wade system, usually in order to represent the local dialect pronunciation. Thus Bishop Kaung's *(cow* plus *ng)* spelling represents the Shanghai dialect pronunciation, and S. C. Leung's *(lee-ung)* the Cantonese. Watchman Nyi's surname is pronounced *nee*. Helen Djang chooses a more phonetic spelling than the standard Wade spelling of *chang*.

Note that the surname regularly comes first, except when the name has been westernized by the use of initials or a Western given name. Thus Wu Yao-tsung is known to most of his Western friends as Y. T. Wu.

NOTE ON TRANSLATIONS

All translations from Chinese sources were made by the author except for the English version of the Christian Manifesto (p. 51), which was prepared by the Chinese leaders who issued it.

Contents

Contents

A Crisis in Mission

Foreign Missions in Battle Array[1]

An endless line of splendor,
These troops with heaven for home,
With creeds they go from Scotland,
With incense go from Rome.
These in the name of Jesus
Against the dark gods stand,
They gird the earth with valor,
They heed their King's command.

Onward the line advances,
Shaking the hills with power,
Slaying the hidden demons,
The lions that devour.
No bloodshed in the wrestling—
But souls new-born arise—
The nations growing kinder,
The child-hearts growing wise.

[1] Vachel Lindsay in *Collected Poems*. (New York: The Macmillan Company, 1913.) Used with their permission.

> What is the final ending?
> The issue, can we know?
> Will Christ outlive Mohammed?
> Will Kali's altar go?
> This is our faith tremendous,
> Our wild hope, who shall scorn,
> That in the name of Jesus
> The world shall be reborn.

This poem by Vachel Lindsay is an admirable expression of the romantic idealism that has led Christian missionaries out to the ends of the earth. And although the last stanza recognizes that the final outcome is a matter of faith rather than knowledge, still the second stanza can confidently picture the whole process as one of steady advance. Are we justified in this expectation?

We remember that St. Augustine lived and died, and made his great contribution to Christian theology, within the confines of the church of North Africa—a church that, along with its sister churches in the Near East, was completely blotted out less than three centuries later by the new force of a militant Islam. This defection from Christendom was so serious that Latourette could label the period from 500 to 1500 as "The Thousand Years of Uncertainty." It was a whole millennium in which Muslim power seemed to belie the Christian hope to become a faith and a way of life for all mankind.

It is to be noted that this millennium saw three separate and protracted attempts to establish Christianity in China, all of which failed completely. The Nestorian Church gained a footing in China during the T'ang Dynasty (618-907) but lost it before the end of that dynasty. The Nestorians tried again during the Mongol Dynasty (1280-1368), a period that also witnessed the establishment of Roman Catholic churches in various parts of the empire. These last two attempts were also blotted out by the resurgence of a vigorous isolationist nationalism in the succeeding Ming Dynasty.

During the next four centuries, the Christian church regained the initiative and made important advances that brought it into almost every country in the world. Such was the situation that led Vachel Lindsay to paint the optimistic picture presented in his poem.

Now in the twentieth century, Christianity finds itself confronted with a new and still more formidable defection, the militant atheism of organized communism. Wherever communism comes to power, the Christian church is in trouble. In Russia the proud and ancient Russian Orthodox Church has sunk to a shadow of what it once was. The churches in East Germany, Czechoslovakia, and Hungary have not yet suffered as the Russian Orthodox Church has, but what will they be like when they have lived under a Communist regime for forty years?

If it is so difficult for an old established church just to maintain itself in the face of Communist atheism, what hope may we have for the "younger churches," churches with no long tradition of Christian life to hold their loyalty? If these young churches are subjected to a long period of Communist domination, will they be able to maintain even

3

a bare existence, or must we reconcile ourselves to seeing them blotted out completely?

The Chinese church is one of the first of the younger churches to be subjected to Communist domination, and so its experience forms a sort of test case on this critical question. If with some adjustment and compromise it can continue to exist and bear witness to the gospel, then there is hope that younger churches in other parts of the world who may later face the same experience will also be able to survive. And if we find that there have been mistakes in mission policy that have aggravated the situation for the church in China and made its survival under the new conditions more difficult, there may still be time to correct those mistakes in the other countries where a mission proclamation of the gospel is going on.

But we are interested in China for its own sake, and not just for what its experience can tell us about our work in other places. China is a mighty giant, with by far the largest population of any country on earth, with the longest continuous culture that the world has ever seen, and with ancient achievements in philosophy and the arts that compare favorably with the best produced anywhere in world history. For long China has lain weak and ineffective, but now its latent energies are being focused on a program of social reconstruction that is rapidly bringing it to the forefront among modern nations. It already exerts a commanding influence in the Far East and is increasingly a force to be reckoned with on the world scene.

However, American concern for the future of the Chinese

Christian church is a concern that transcends the immediacies of political issues. The traditional friendship between the two countries brought during the past century an ever greater involvement of American churches in the developing life of the Chinese church. Throughout the whole of this century, there have been more missionaries to China from the United States than from all the rest of the world. And in a reverse flow, American colleges and universities have welcomed Chinese students, and these have forged a still closer bond of friendship between the two countries through the years.

Even apart from these special ties of friendship, there has been a growing recognition of the Chinese church as a part of Christ's body, the Church Universal. At the International Missionary Council's Madras Conference in 1938, the Chinese delegation took the lead among the representatives of the younger churches and impressed the world with the vigor of its thought and the depth of its commitment to the Christian gospel. Worthy representatives of the Chinese church, such as Y.M.C.A. Secretary T. Z. Koo, Methodist Bishop W. Y. Ch'en, Yenching University Professor T. C. Chao, and Huachung University President Francis Wei have toured American churches, speaking with a maturity of thought and depth of insight that have invariably made a deep impression upon their hearers. When the World Council of Churches was organized in Amsterdam in 1948, one of this number, Dr. T. C. Chao, was made one of the six presidents of the Council. This act shows a world-wide recognition that the church in China is a full partner with the other churches of the world in the common task of Christian witness.

For all of these reasons, there is a deep and abiding interest among Americans in the fate of the Christian church in China. The withdrawal of all missionaries and consequent lack of firsthand information, and also the exaggeration of Communist excesses reported in the American press, have led many to the mistaken conclusion that the church is already finished in China.

The following account is intended to correct that impression by presenting a picture of a church striving to adapt itself to its new situation in such a way that it may continue to preach the way of salvation through Christ. Is it fighting a losing battle, or will it succeed in establishing a point of vantage from which it may gradually permeate the life of the new China with the Christian spirit? The world does not yet have the answer to this question, and it may be concluded from the account that follows that the issue is still in the balance. The Chinese church is still in a period of crisis. The situation is full of danger, but it is also full of opportunity for the years ahead.

The Church in 1949

On a bright April day in 1949, I stood on a street in Nanking and watched a detachment of victorious Communist troops swing down the street. They had just crossed the Yangtze River and were now in process of occupying the city that, except for the wartime interlude, had been the proud capital of the Nationalist Chinese government since 1927.

How completely this event marked the end of one era and the beginning of a new one, we were not fully aware at that time. Those of us who were old-timers in China, and had seen one army and one regime being replaced by another so many times, may perhaps be excused if at that time we thought this was just another in the succession of military coups. We did not see it for what it really was—a dividing line in Chinese history as definitive as the Exile was in Old Testament history. Just as Old Testament events are dated as pre-exilic, exilic, or post-exilic, so events in modern Chinese history were destined to be dated as before or after the event that the Communists call "Liberation"—the establishment of a Communist government in mainland China.

This was a complete revolution in which all the old established patterns of collective and individual living were to be broken up and remolded—remade into the Marxist pattern. And this revolution, which was so mightily to affect the economic life, the social customs, the education and culture of China, could not be expected to leave untouched the religious life of the little Christian churches scattered throughout the country.

Christian Beginnings

Christians in China were a small minority of the population. In a country that, as a later Communist census was to show us, was approaching 600 million people, Roman Catholic Christians numbered about 3 million and Protestant Christians about 1 million, a total of less than 1 per cent of the population. It is true that the Christian gospel had made a far deeper impression upon China than these figures might indicate, for the leavening influence of Christian ideals had spread far beyond the bounds of the churches themselves. Nonetheless, the church remained very much of a minority movement, in spite of three and a half centuries of Roman Catholic missions and a century and a half of Protestant missions, whose scope and intensity were unparalleled anywhere else in religious history.

The Roman Catholic missionary effort had continued unbroken from the time of Matteo Ricci, who established residence in China in 1583, right down to this year of destiny 1949. The result was a firmly rooted Chinese Catholic church covering the whole country, and including in its hierarchy a Chinese cardinal, 20 archbishops, about 140 bishops, a large number of whom were Chinese, and some 2000 priests.

This church did not supplement its evangelistic efforts with as much in the way of hospitals and schools as Protestant missionaries regularly did, but still in 1949 it had three universities of high quality—Aurora University in Shanghai, Fu Jen University in Peking, and Tsinku University in Tientsin—as well as a considerable number of schools on the elementary and secondary levels. Orphanages were a more characteristic expression of the Catholic outreach, and down through the years these institutions saved the lives of countless thousands of abandoned children.

The Protestant churches of the West did not begin their missionary endeavors in China until the year 1807, when Robert Morrison arrived in China under the auspices of the London Missionary Society. Missionary effort remained scattered and sporadic until after the year 1842, when the Treaty of Nanking—following the Opium War between China and Great Britain—opened up the ports of Canton, Amoy, Foochow, Ningpo, and Shanghai to foreign residence. The major portion of the Protestant missionary endeavor, therefore, had a duration of only about a hundred years before its activities were brought to a close by the Communist triumph.

THE CHURCH IN COMMUNIST CHINA

Protestant Unity

The degree of unity of spirit and purpose achieved by Protestant churches by the year 1949 was very remarkable. It is true, of course, that the number of separate and independent agencies at work in China reached literally into the hundreds, and each was intent on reproducing in China the type of church life from which it had come in the West—indeed, what missionary is qualified to do otherwise? But the very immensity of the task, the self-sufficiency of the ancient Chinese culture, and the apparent hopelessness of the attempt to make in it a place for Christian thought, all combined to bring missionaries of different denominations together in a unity of spirit and purpose beyond that achieved by their sending churches.

One instance of this co-operation can be seen in the comity agreements that missionaries regularly entered into. If the missionaries of two or more different denominations found themselves living in the same large city, they would meet and agree on the directions from that central city for which each would assume responsibility. In this way, Nanking Methodists took the road leading southwest to Wuhu; Presbyterians, the road leading southeast toward Huchow.

These comity agreements were hailed at the time as a notable advance in denominational co-operation, which they actually were. One would look in vain for any similar mutual consideration by the competing churches of a century ago in America, England, or the continent. But the inevitable, although apparently unconsidered, result of those agreements was the development of the Chinese church along a curious, crazy quilt pattern of denominational loyalties. How the new church would develop a regional fellowship and what would happen in any population shift—these were questions that were not grappled with because of the denominational limitations of those days.

If denominational differences within Protestantism often seem to us in the West as illogical and unchristian, they become far more so when they are separated from their original historical and geographical occasions and arbitrarily assigned to limited districts side by side in a foreign land. It is well to keep the unfortunate nature of this missionary heritage in mind as we come to see what the Chinese church has been doing since it has been separated from direct missionary influence.

Western Denominations in China

One would naturally expect the different branches of the same denomination to gravitate together, but it is interesting to note that it was those churches that historically had the inclusive ideal of the state church in their background that were the most successful in achieving integration. Take, for example, the Anglican Communion. There were originally separate and independent missionary efforts by four different mission societies from England, one from Canada, one from Australia, and one from the United States. In 1912 all the churches developed by these missions, plus some that had been developed by Anglicans in the China

11

Inland Mission in eastern Szechuan, were amalgamated into one independent church, the Chung Hua Sheng Kung Hui (Holy Catholic Church of China; Chung Hua, meaning China, is sometimes omitted). This church is recognized by the Archbishop of Canterbury and the Lambeth Conference as a part of the world-wide Anglican Communion. In 1949 it had fourteen dioceses and a reported membership of 76,741.

However, even here, the union, while real as far as it went, was not very deep. When we consider how important the one prayer book is as a unifying influence in the Protestant Episcopal Church in America, or in the Anglican Church, we may be startled to know that the Chung Hua Sheng Kung Hui, from its organization in 1912 to the fateful year of 1949, had never succeeded in getting a uniform prayer book for its various sections. Each section still continued the use of the separate prayer book it had prepared before the merger. More recently, Bishop T. K. Shen was commissioned to edit a uniform prayer book for use by the whole of the Sheng Kung Hui. Whether it has been published as yet is not known.

The Lutheran Church also stems from a state church background. There were some fifteen or twenty separate Lutheran mission boards at work in China, several from America and the rest from the Lutheran countries of Europe. Representatives of a number of these got together in 1917 and organized the Lutheran Church of China, with the expressive name in Chinese of Hsin I Hui (The Faith Righteousness Church). This church has its strongest work in the central provinces of Hunan, Hupeh, and Honan, and in Kwangtung, Shantung, and in what was Manchuria. Statistics published in 1951 give it 83,126 members and 19,928 catechumens, for a total constituency of 103,054.

This union is not as complete as that of the Anglicans, for there have been several Lutheran churches that have refused to join the Hsin I Hui. Moreover, in 1949 the sixteen synods of this church still corresponded exactly with the areas of work of the sixteen founding mission boards, though in a number of cases a modification or merger would have seemed logical after the organization of a united church.

The Church of Christ in China, to the extent to which it reflects the Presbyterian and Reformed church traditions, also has something of a state church background. This church, however, represents a much wider union. Besides Presbyterian and Reformed Churches, it includes most Congregational Churches (all except the North China Congregational Church), the English Baptists, the United Church of Canada, the United Brethren in Christ, and even one conference of the Methodist Church. The union was effected by a series of steps that reached culmination in 1927 and made the Church of Christ in China the largest Protestant church in the nation as well as the most widely inclusive, for it reached into almost every province. Its membership, as reported in 1949, was 176,983. In addition there was a continuing Presbyterian Church, with a 1949 membership reported at thirty thousand, that entered this church after "Liberation."

A vigorous central secretaryship had succeeded in bringing a certain amount of unity and nation-wide fellowship to the Church of Christ in China, although in many ways it too was more of a loose federation of the original diverse elements than an organic unity.

Eight different Methodist mission boards, three from Great Britain, four from the United States, and one from Canada, had been successful in building up large and vigorous churches in China. But for some reason, the impulse toward unity was never strong enough to bring any of these groups together by their own initiative. The three British churches finally united at home in 1932, and three of the four American churches (all except the Free Methodist) united in 1939. These unions, of course, automatically unified their constituent churches in China. The Canadian Methodists went by way of the United Church of Canada into the Church of Christ in China, and the Free Methodist Church continued as a tiny separate body.

The two large Methodist bodies undoubtedly would have gotten together in time into one church. Indeed, in 1947 and 1948, active negotiations were in process looking toward that end, but the attempt came to nothing. The new era found the Methodists divided into the Wei Li Kung Hui of American background and the Shun Tao Kung Hui of British background. In 1949 the Wei Li Kung Hui had a membership of 102,693, and the Shun Tao Kung Hui counted 44,410 members. If they could have gotten together they would have had a church with work in thirteen of the provinces of China, and thus would have qualified more clearly as a nation-wide church body.

14

Similarly, the two large conventions of churches founded by North American Baptists, though co-operating in various institutions, such as Shanghai University, were never able to get together as one denomination. The year 1949 found them as two separate churches, the Chin Hsin Hui of Southern Baptist background with 65,000 members, and the Chin Li Hui of Northern Baptist derivation with 16,701 members. By this time the English Baptists had found a home in the Church of Christ in China. The Swedish Baptists had developed a strong church in Shantung Province. A natural Baptist merger might have been to unite with the Disciples Church centering in Nanking, but this was never accomplished.

Other smaller denominations brought in from the West, to name those with membership of ten thousand or over in 1949, include the Christian and Missionary Alliance, the Seventh-day Adventists, and the Assemblies of God.

One of the most remarkable denominations in China is the church developed by the China Inland Mission. This organization, founded by Hudson Taylor, is thought of in the West as an interdenominational agency, and it draws support and missionaries from all the major Protestant denominations. It has home offices in England, America, and Australia and is affiliated with similar agencies in the Protestant countries of Europe.

The general plan of the CIM has been to group missionaries of the same denominational background in the same area, with the expectation that the church developed there should also be of that denomination. This has actually worked out in some areas, notably in Szechuan Province, where, as noted previously, the CIM Anglican missionaries developed a church that is now a part of the Chung Hua Sheng Kung Hui. However, geographical separation and the difficulties of travel, as well as the pietistic indifference to church organization that is characteristic of the CIM, have usually prevented fellowship of CIM churches with like denominations in other parts of the country. The result has been the formation of regional federations that are known as the Nei Ti Hui (China Inland Mission Churches). In 1949 they reported 86,345 members. This mission, though also strong in East China, always has chosen the more remote areas to evangelize as a matter of policy. The farther west you went in China, into the mountainous regions difficult of access, the more apt you were to find there no mission board except the CIM at work.

Indigenous Churches

One outstanding feature of the generation preceding 1949 was the development of indigenous Chinese churches. This took place on such a scale that by 1949 they made up about 25 per cent of the numerical strength of Protestant Christianity. These churches began largely by withdrawals from the older denominations, but they then developed their own evangelistic outreach. By 1949 a considerable proportion of their members had come into their fellowship directly, and not by way of the Western churches.

The most widespread of these churches was the True Jesus Church, established by Paul Wei in 1917. In that year, having been deeply moved by the Holy Spirit, Paul Wei sold all his possessions and went out to preach the gospel. He established the first True Jesus Church in Tientsin, and then one in Peking. One of his earliest adherents was Barnabas Chang of Shantung. Barnabas established a True Jesus Church in Weihsien and practiced communal living, following the example of the early apostolic church. The movement spread to other provinces, and even outside China to the Chinese living in the South Seas, Korea, Japan, and Honolulu. There are now over a thousand organized congregations of this denomination, with over a hundred thousand members. The church emphasizes the literal interpretation of the Bible, faith healing, and ecstatic utterance, but the communal living feature of the founders has not been continued.

The next largest of the indigenous sects is popularly known as the Little Flock, but their own name for themselves is Christian Meeting Places, a name indicative of their opposition to formal church organization. The first of these was organized by Watchman Nyi in 1926, with evangelism as its main emphasis. By 1949 it had more than seven hundred churches, with a membership of over seventy thousand. Its church polity is strongly congregational, so that it never had any central office. It has no ordained ministry.

The most colorful of the new denominations was the Jesus Family founded by Ching Tien-ying. He came as a young man to the Methodist school in Taian, Shantung, with the avowed purpose of converting these foreigners to

Buddhism. Instead, he was himself converted to Christianity, largely through the efforts of Miss Nora Dillenbeck and Miss Lillian Greer. These two women were inclined toward a very ecstatic expression of religious emotion, which fitted in exactly with Ching Tien-ying's temperament. This spirit spread like wildfire among the Methodist churches of Shantung, and they were recalled by church authorities to a more conventional expression of Christian faith only with difficulty.

In the meantime, Ching Tien-ying organized his first communal Christian society in the little village of Machuang, Shantung, in 1921. Everyone who came into the Family turned over all his property and then lived and worked under the direction of the Family head. As new communities were organized, a head would be appointed for each one, but Ching Tien-ying remained in general charge of all the communities, as well as being the head of the mother community in Machuang. His control was very tight, extending to such things as the direction of daily work and decisions on the marriage of Family members. By 1949, 141 different communities had been organized in 8 provinces, the larger number of them in the province of Shantung, with perhaps 6,000 members.

The Jesus Family members were a hard-working and practical people. Among them were technicians capable of installing electric light plants, and doctors and nurses able to run a modern hospital. They spent five or six hours a day in prayer and worship, and seven or eight hours a day in work. As they worked they sang simple songs of their own

18

composing, some based on Bible imagery, as "The Song of the Ark" or "A Crumb of Heavenly Yeast," others using the favorite Chinese device of counting, such as "The Twenty Sorrows of Jesus" or "The Ten Fools."

There are two different sects in China with the word Independent in their names: China Jesus Independent Church and China Christian Independent Church. Unwary commentators are constantly confusing the two, but they are quite distinct denominations. The former began as a revolt against missionary domination of the church in Shanghai. The first stages in the movement reach back to 1906, when Pastor Yu Kuo-chen started the revolt. This church has grown largely through withdrawals from the older churches. It has spread out from Shanghai, especially through the provinces of Chekiang and Fukien, and now has about three hundred congregations. If we can assume that these congregations average about a hundred each, then this would be a church of about thirty thousand members. Its present leader is the Rev. Hsieh Yung-ch'in of Shanghai.

The other Independent Church was organized in Shantung in 1912, and this one, instead of being a revolt against missionary control, was organized with missionary co-operation and encouragement. When the Church of Christ in China was formed, many congregations of this sect entered the new union. Now the China Christian Independent Church is of rather minor proportions.

Among the more recently established indigenous sects are the Spiritual Food Church and the Spiritual Work

Church. The former was organized by the Rev. Chao Shih-kuang, with some help from a Christian and Missionary Alliance missionary.

In addition to all the above, there were a great many small and unconnected groups scattered throughout the country. For example, the Salvation Army reported a membership of over four thousand in 1935, and there were many other similarly small groups—Mennonites, Quakers, Christian Advent Mission, to name a few. These groups were too small to form an effective church, and yet they were unwilling to become a part of one of the larger churches.

Supporting Institutions

The evangelistic efforts of all these churches were supplemented by an elaborate system of supporting institutions. There were theological and Bible schools for the training of Christian workers, of which the most outstanding were the Yenching School of Religion at Peking, Nanking Theological Seminary, and Canton Union Theological College. There was a China Bible House, which co-ordinated the efforts of the British, Scotch, and American Bible Societies. The China Bible House promoted the distribution of a very fine translation of the Bible into the national language, as well as a considerable number of dialect versions. There was a National Christian Council of evergrowing effectiveness that served to underline the essential unity of the whole Protestant enterprise in China, in spite of its apparent fragmentariness. There were book concerns devoted to the publishing of Christian literature, chief of which were the Christian Literature Society and the Association Press of the Y.M.C.A. And every large city had its Young Men's and Young Women's Christian Associations.

Most important of all, church work was supplemented by a nation-wide array of schools and hospitals—institutions in which the Christian spirit of service was made more concrete. More than two hundred Christian hospitals scattered throughout the country were pioneers in bringing the benefits of modern medicine to the Chinese people. The capstone of this health service was the truly magnificent Peking Union Medical College, a combination medical school and hospital originated by missions and then taken over by the Rockefeller Foundation. It was developed into one of the outstanding medical centers of the world.

The Christian school system ranged all the way from kindergartens to universities. All the pioneer missionaries had found it necessary to open primary schools, for at that time there was no state-supported education whatever in China. The next natural step was the opening of high schools (called middle schools in China, they numbered about two hundred in 1949), and finally, in the early years of this century, the great system of Christian colleges and universities began to emerge. Since the support of a modern university was usually too great a burden for a single mission board to undertake, the majority of these schools were union institutions. Several mission boards working in a given area would join together in the establishment and administration of the school, thus emphasizing still more to the world at large the essential unity of the Protestant missionary enterprise. By 1949 these thirteen Christian colleges and universities had sent out over fifty thousand graduates, most of whom, of course, are still living and working in China.

This then was the picture in 1949, when the Communists came to power. Behind all the façade of foreign missionary help there was a growing but still infant Chinese church. What chance did it have to survive when the whole missionary apparatus was snatched away? Not only the larger number of supporting institutions, but even many of the smaller local churches required missionary aid in order to carry on. Now, that aid was to be taken away, and this young church, with limited experience in standing alone, was to find itself under a government that scoffed at religion (calling it "the opiate of the people") and refrained from a frontal attack upon the church only because it was convinced that the church and all religion would die away of itself under the conditions of a Communist state. Was the faith of this young church deep enough, mature enough to meet victoriously the difficulties of this new period? This is a question to which the final answer has not yet been given, but perhaps the succeeding chapters of this book will give us some ground for at least a tentatively affirmative answer.

China Under Communism

The growth of the Chinese Communist party is one of the amazing phenomena of modern times. It was organized by a little group of men meeting in an upstairs room of a house in Shanghai in 1921. Two years later the group decided to infiltrate Sun Yat Sen's Nationalist party, based in Canton. In 1926 Nationalist armies, under Chiang Kai-shek, began to march north to unify the disorganized country, and by the following spring the Communist wing had grown strong enough to dominate the Nationalist government set up in Hankow. When this government was repudiated by Chiang Kai-shek, the Communist party established itself in Kiangsi Province, maintained itself there for several years, and then made the famous Long March to Northwest China (1934-35), where it made a new center for itself in northern Shensi Province, with Yenan as its capital. There its power steadily increased.

During the war with Japan, the Communists mastered the technique of guerilla warfare behind the Japanese lines, and

23

thus stole a march over the more stolid and conventional Nationalist government. By the end of the war in 1945 the Communist armies had attained a commanding position over much of North China. Finally, after the breakdown of General Marshall's endeavors to work out a compromise between the two parties, the issue was joined in civil war. The Nationalist government, though generously supported by American war matériel and a large American military advisory unit, collapsed like a house of cards. The Communist armies, after occupying the Nationalist capital of Nanking in April 1949, spread out over the rest of China just about as fast as their armies could march, without meeting any effective opposition anywhere. The Nationalist government was pushed off the mainland onto the island of Taiwan (Formosa), where it has been able to maintain itself only with the protection of the American Seventh Fleet and extensive financial assistance.

What caused the Nationalist government to collapse so swiftly and so utterly? The causes are not to be found in any action, or failure to act, on the part of the United States or any other external government, but are rather to be sought within China herself. By 1949 the Nationalist government seemed to many Chinese to have "lost the mandate of Heaven," first, because of its bumbling ineffectiveness in meeting the postwar problems of reconstruction and in particular the inflation crisis; and again, because in the face of the Communist threat, it found itself hopelessly rent by internal factions. In the minds of many thoughtful Chinese, the Nationalist party had been tried and found wanting for a long period of time, and they were willing to let it go.

Another reason for the rapid Communist success may be the Communist land reform propaganda. In a country that is largely agrarian, it was inevitable that both of the contending armies, the Nationalist and the Communist, should be composed almost entirely of farm boys. When the farm boys in the Nationalist armies were persuaded that their fathers and uncles back home would be better off under a Communist regime that would reform the whole landlord system, their natural reaction was, "Why should we risk our lives to keep in power a regime we would be better off without?" The result was the complete collapse of Nationalist army morale.

This emphasis upon land reform in Communist propaganda led many observers to regard the Chinese Communist party not as a true Communist party at all but as merely a party of agrarian reformers. The Communists themselves were not averse to letting that picture prevail, and, in fact, presented themselves in that guise as long as it served the purpose of softening up any opposition that the prospect of a true Communist regime might have aroused. But as soon as victory had been achieved, Mao Tse-tung lost no time in proclaiming the true unity of the new regime with Soviet Russia and the rest of the Communist world. We "lean to one side," he said. That is, we are not trying to maintain a neutral position between the Communist world and the non-Communist world, but are frankly aligning ourselves with the former.

25

THE CHURCH IN COMMUNIST CHINA

The People's Republic of China was formally inaugurated in Peking on October 1, 1949. Ever since then, that date has been Independence Day for mainland China in contrast to October 10 (Double Tenth), which is celebrated by the Nationalists in commemoration of the Revolution in 1911. The comparative popularity of the two regimes in places outside China, such as Hong Kong, can be gauged by the difference in noisiness of the firecracker demonstrations on those two days. In Hong Kong, after two or three uncertain years, the October 10 celebration has decisively won out.

The new masters of China were not unduly precipitate in inaugurating Marxist reforms. Even as late as November 1950, when the writer left China, there had been no fundamental change in the ownership of land, shops, or banks. The one change that did begin promptly in every place the Communists occupied was the organization of study classes or lecture programs for indoctrination. Every level of urban society was brought into this comprehensive "educational" campaign. College professors, with Ph.D. degrees from American universities, had to go back to school to listen to lectures on Marxism. At the other end of the intellectual scale, such groups as ricksha pullers were organized into classes that met once or twice a week. These groups were lectured on the superiority of the new system, a system in which they, the down-trodden, could now begin to acquire economic equality with the rest of society. On the whole, the leadership of these classes was competent and persuasive, and well graded to the intellectual level of the various classes. While there were many who did not take too readily to the new ideas, there seemed to have been comparatively few who felt that their new teachers did not know what they were talking about.

Land Reform

The Communists had come to power on the issue of land reform, and land reform was the first extensive application of the socialist principle that they undertook. For a year and a half they laid the groundwork, dividing the land into convenient-sized districts for administration, gathering information about all who belonged to the landlord class, and studying the local population to find the natural leaders who could be brought in to help administer the redistribution.

For every administrative district, they usually appointed a committee of from fifteen to twenty persons, the majority of which were local peasants of the landless class. Two or three seasoned Communists directed operations, and several of the intelligentsia from some nearby city were included. The latter would be able to do the paper work involved and at the same time would be given experience in the application of Communist ideas. It is noteworthy that in the choice of local peasants for this committee the new rulers of China were quite willing to use illiterates and even women as long as they had a good reputation among their fellow-villagers. The standard procedure in these committees, undoubtedly with many local variations, was as follows:

27

The first thing on the agenda was the dispossession of all the landlords in the district. If any of them had at any time within the past twenty or more years treated their tenants with harshness or cruelty, they would be brought to trial. If convicted, they would be sentenced to death or imprisonment, or at least fined heavily—usually enough to render them penniless—and thereafter subjected to constant discrimination. Initially the Communist attitude toward landlords was extremely harsh, considering that a landlord *ipso facto* was considered worthy of death. But in the nation-wide redistribution program of 1951 and 1952, this attitude was mitigated, and the majority of landlords were probably let off with the loss of their property and reduction to the economic level of their tenants. In the news items of later years, one frequently reads of the activities of individuals who are identified as "former landlords," thus indicating that not all of them were done to death. The assumption in the West that all landlords were slaughtered has led to exaggerated estimates of the bloodshed of that period. The actual facts were bad enough—informed estimates vary from two to five million including bandits, Nationalist remnants, counter-revolutionaries, and others—but nothing like the twenty million executions reported in some American magazines.

Farmers with a small piece of land that they worked themselves, not hiring any laborers, were usually left unmolested.

The next step was the listing of all the landless in the district. The amount of land available for distribution and the number of persons among whom it was to be distributed were then correlated, after which the land was divided up into the requisite number of individual plots. Finally, the climax of the whole program was the assignment of a plot to each person. To insure fairness, the assignment was supposed to be by lot, but it is hard to imagine that politically worthy individuals did not get special consideration. The land assignment was confirmed by the actual issuance of deeds, a step of great symbolic value to a peasant who all his life had been landless, working fields that belonged to someone else. Usually he did not reflect that a government that could take the land away from the former owners could also take it away from its new owners.

This land redistribution was purely a temporary step, the purpose of which was to gain the support of the peasants in the early consolidation period and to achieve the complete liquidation of the landlord class. The redistribution simply replaced a few big landowners by a great many small landowners. Anyone conversant with Communist theory would know that the process would not stop there. Actually, however, the peasants were given some three or four years to savor the sweetness of land ownership before the Communist government felt ready to start the new dispossession process.

Reconstruction in accordance with Marxist theory proceeds through the stage of socialization to the final stage of a Communist order. The changes described here are all in what Communists call the socialization stage.

The first step in the socialization process was the organization of mutual aid teams. That is, a score or more of peasant families, each family retaining its own plot of land, would be brought together for mutual help in seeding and harvest, for local irrigation projects, and the like. The next step was the organization of small co-operatives, where the ownership of the land itself would be tacitly surrendered to the group, though the return to the individual would still be graded to some extent on the property he had put into the pool. Then came the large co-operatives, where the holdings of several hundred families would be pooled for joint operation. By this time the return to the individual was no longer based upon any former property holding, but was based entirely upon the work credits he achieved, a system in which skilled labor received a somewhat higher rating than unskilled.

The final step was the grouping together of thirty or forty of these co-operatives to form a commune. A typical commune might have as many as five thousand families in it. This ultimate in co-operation took place in 1958 and has been widely publicized in the West because of the initial extremes to which it went. Now land ownership and the administrative and accounting unit have been returned to the level of the large co-operative, which has been renamed a production brigade.

One new and significant element has been introduced into the payment to commune members. In the preceding stages the principle "To each according to his labor" was followed. Now this has been modified by what is called the Communist principle "To each according to his need." In some communes, not all, the families of the members eat free of charge in the public mess halls, thus reducing the

30

cash return to the worker. In this way, the man with a large family gets a greater return for his labor than the single man.

The main reason for the wide publicity given in the West to the organization of the commune is the fact that it coincided with new measures looking toward the liquidation of the family as an economic unit. Family meals were transferred to public mess halls, the care of children to public nurseries and kindergartens, and laundry, house cleaning, mending of clothes, and numerous other housekeeping chores to service teams. As a result, millions of women who formerly gave their whole time to their homes have been "liberated" from household drudgery and are now "free" to spend their days in "happy productivity" in fields or factories.

This whole process of socialization of the land has not taken place smoothly and easily. We have already noted the bloodshed accompanying the liquidation of the landlord class. A few years later the widespread opposition of the peasants, when they began to realize that they, too, were about to be dispossessed, caused a serious dislocation in the agricultural program. The peasants could not do anything about the fields that they had to turn over to the co-operatives, but their livestock was a different matter. All over China the peasants offered their draft bullocks and their hogs for sale to the butcher rather than turn them in for nothing to the co-operative. The animals became a glut on the market, and the price of meat reached an all-time low. But the only result of this maneuver was to make things harder for the peasants themselves. When the co-operatives

31

found themselves without enough bullocks to do the plowing, their only recourse was to hitch the peasants to the plows.

Again, the mess halls have been a favorite point of attack for Chinese complainers. Throughout 1959 and 1960 the press took cognizance of the discontent by constant promises to improve the mess halls. In some places the outcry was so great that the Communist cadres gave up in despair and allowed the peasants to re-establish their own kitchens. The press, however, uniformly condemned this procedure, demanding that the abandoned mess halls be revived. In the spring of 1959, and again in the spring of 1960, many mess halls ran out of food and had to shut down.

Socialization of Industry

The socialization process in industry and commerce followed a different pattern. Here the main problem was how to keep the services of a greater part of the managerial talent while gradually taking away their prerogatives. This was accomplished by two parallel courses of action; one directed at individuals, the other toward control of business enterprises. First, as in the treatment of the landlords, the minority of more stubborn businessmen were so severely punished that the rest were thoroughly cowed.

For the purpose of control, the Five-anti Campaign was inaugurated. The Five-anti Campaign was the third great denunciation movement of the early years of the Communist regime. The first was the liquidation of the landlords. Then in the latter part of 1951 came a Three-anti Campaign, directed against corruption, decay, and bureaucratism in the ranks of government workers. It was officially announced that 4.5 per cent of governmental personnel suffered punishment in this campaign, but the number probably was greater than that. Next, in the spring of 1952, came the Five-anti Campaign against businessmen—a campaign against the five "poisons" of bribery, tax evasion, fraud, theft of government property, and theft of state economic secrets. These five crimes were interpreted in such a broad way that it was possible to convict practically any businessman the government wished to single out. The result was a reign of terror and panic among businessmen. It was reported that 76 per cent of the 450,000 businessmen investigated in seven leading cities had been found guilty of one or more of these crimes. Some were sentenced to prison terms or death, but the majority were let off with the payment of heavy fines or the confiscation of all their property. As a result of this extraordinary income, the government was able, in spite of the heavy expenses of the Korean War, to end the year 1952 with a surplus.

The second course of action taken toward the socialization of industry and commerce was a graduated series of steps controlling and manipulating raw materials, transportation, and markets. This was done in such a way as to bring every enterprise to virtual bankruptcy. But businesses were not allowed to go bankrupt, for under the guise of protecting the workingman, the government forbade any concern to close its doors or reduce its work force. When a company's reserves were all used up and it appealed to the government for relief, it found a sympathetic hearing and a practical proposal for meeting the situation: Keep the present management, but make the government a 50 per cent joint owner of the company. The government then would be able to iron out any difficulties in regard to raw materials, transportation, or markets that had caused the company to lose money. In this way all business concerns in the country became joint public-private concerns, a situation that continued until 1956. At that time, in a great socialization campaign, the businessmen were led to surrender their half of the ownership completely and take on the status of managers of completely government-owned concerns.

Accordingly, when the commune movement came along in 1958, the public ownership of all business concerns had been established to the complete satisfaction of the government, and no further change in that relationship was required. As a result, the later city commune is a less significant economic development than the country commune. The latter is at least indirectly related to the fundamental means of production, namely, the land, through the ownership of it by the production brigade. But the big industrial plants and commercial establishments around which the city commune has been organized are quite independent of it. The economic purpose of the city commune is to mobilize the labor capacity of housewives for various supplementary types of production. Small neighborhood factories have been established, and these absorb the labor of the women who have been freed from the home by the organization of mess halls and nurseries and service teams. Whether this extreme of collective living will find any greater degree of acceptance in the cities than it has in the rural areas remains to be seen.

One of the points of strength in the development of the country and city communes has been the almost mystic sense, reflected in all the literature, that in this social structure they are finally approaching pure communism, where the Communist ideal of "From each according to his ability, to each according to his need" may find complete expression. There is evidence, however, that the famine conditions of 1960-61 have brought considerable disillusionment.

Communist Morale

The Communist party has shown a surprising unity throughout this whole process. In the Three-anti Campaign many minor officials were purged, but no wrongdoing has been reported in any of the higher echelons. The only incident that resembles the violent purges periodically required in the Communist party of Russia was the denunciation in 1955 of Kao Kang and Jao Shu-shih, two high officials of Northeast China who, though professing loyalty to Mao Tse-tung, were charged with too much independence in their administration of the northeast provinces. After the denunciation, Kao committed suicide and Jao is presumably either in prison or dead, but his trial and sentence have never been reported. It is undoubtedly the high prestige of Mao Tse-tung that has prevented the appearance of any serious rifts in the party. At the present time, too, the succession seems to be so definitely in the hands of Liu Shaochi that no upheaval is likely when Mao passes from the scene.

This unity of party command, the completeness of the triumph over the Nationalist government, and the utter absence of any alternative program were the elements that made it possible for the Communists to carry through their economic revolution with such a high hand. The lack of effective opposition led them to misjudge the degree of their popularity among the people, and in 1956 they invited a period of open criticism. In two speeches, May 1956 and February 1957, Mao Tse-tung used the famous phrase, "Let a hundred flowers bloom. Let a hundred schools contend." Previously, the people sometimes had had difficulty in fulfilling the quotas assigned to them by their government taskmasters, but this time they overfulfilled their quota. The flood of criticism and opposition that was let loose quite appalled the government, which looked upon itself as the liberator and benefactor of a grateful people. The Communist party had expected some such minor criticism as, "I don't like the necktie you are wearing," and were dismayed to hear many of the people saying instead, "I don't like you."

Some people have suspected that the invitation to criticize was a deliberate effort to smoke out any rightists still remaining. But the consensus among observers is that it was a bona fide offer, and that the Communists had been blinded by their own propaganda into thinking that they enjoyed a universal popularity. They now learned that this was not so. A new period of repression and persecution set in during the fall of '57 and all of '58, aimed in particular at those who had been too frank in expressing their views during the brief Hundred Flowers period. The Communist reaction was hailed at first as a Rectification Campaign, in which the government presumably would rectify those mistakes in administration that the criticisms might bring out. Instead, it turned into an antirightist drive, with the criticizers themselves as the object of attack.

This time there was none of the widespread bloodshed that had marked the drives against landlords in the land reform and against businessmen in the Five-anti Campaign, instead there was the "reform through labor program." The government already had ambitious plans afoot to settle the sparsely populated far northwest—Tsinghai and Sinkiang—with tens of thousands of colonists from the overcrowded coastal regions of the east, and so it was a simple matter to condemn the rightists and exile them along with the colonists to some faraway project. Not all of those denounced received this treatment. Some after a brief period of being under a cloud were rehabilitated, but the "reform through labor" device has been so widely used that it has led to the charge that the Communist government has reduced a large segment of its population to slavery.

The year 1958 also saw the inauguration of a tremendous drive to increase production—the Great Leap Forward. Workers were constantly being urged to work faster, hours of work were lengthened, volunteering for extra tasks was

map by palacios

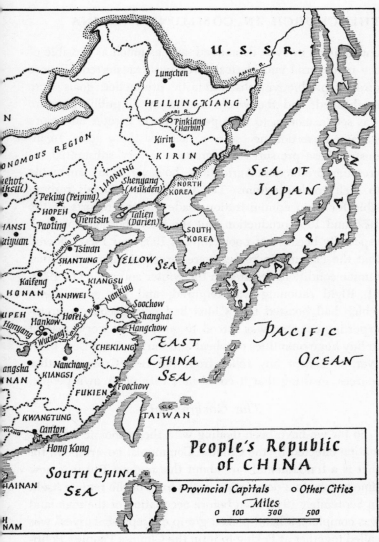

People's Republic
of CHINA

• Provincial Capitals   ○ Other Cities

Miles
0   100   300   500

39

encouraged, or even demanded, and as much as possible of the managerial and clerical force was transferred to more directly productive jobs. Fantastic production goals were established, and the whole machinery of public pressure was set in motion to urge people to the greater and more sustained exertion necessary to achieve those goals. In industry these pressures did produce a very substantial increase in production. Agriculture, however, is less amenable to such crash programs. The Communist officials responsible for farm administration made inflated reports of the 1958 and 1959 production, but the later shortages of food, especially because of poor crops in 1959 and 1960, showed that the claimed increases were largely imaginary. Actual famine conditions resulted in the winter and spring of 1960-61. Rigid rationing was required, and the government, which had boasted that China had now become a grain-exporting country, was forced to go into the world market to buy huge quantities of wheat and barley. It refused, however, to accept any relief from the Red Cross or other sources, insisting that it could take care of its own people.

The Government

So far we have been dealing with the economic transformation effected by the Chinese Communist government, for that is a fundamental fact about this regime. But it is now time to turn to a description of the form of the regime itself. In September 1949, even before occupation of the mainland was complete, a hand-picked group of "representatives" was called together at Peking to form the Chinese People's Political Consultative Conference. The draft of a tentative constitution called the Common Platform, as well as other enabling acts, was presented to them at this time. The approval of the CPPCC to the documents was taken as a formal ratification. As a result of this action, there was set up a series of "people's congresses" on four levels: village, county, province, and national. Election to membership in the village people's congress was directly by the people, to membership in each of the three higher levels by the congresses on the level immediately below it. This election process was carried through for the first time in 1954, and the resulting National People's Congress was constituted on September 15, 1954. As in other Communist countries, the whole process was closely controlled by the Communist party, only one slate of candidates was presented, and the resulting body can therefore hardly be called truly representative of the people. The National People's Congress with 1,226 members is represented when not in session, which is most of the time, by a Standing Committee of 49.

When the first National People's Congress met in 1954, it ratified the draft of a permanent constitution that now replaced the Common Platform of 1949. It is to be noted that both the Common Platform and the Constitution guarantee "freedom of religious belief," though even the most partisan supporters of the regime have admitted that the guarantees often have been violated.

In fairness to a regime that is criticized in the West, it may be pointed out that the system of people's congresses, for all its rigging and control from above, still provides a very considerable training in participation in government. Even the humblest elements in society are duly registered as citizens, and at the proper time called together for discussion of the qualifications of the proposed candidates for public office, after which they are given the opportunity to exercise their franchise by casting their ballots for the preselected candidates. From the standpoint of people accustomed to a secret ballot, this procedure may seem very empty, but it could be the beginning of a training in democracy that will later result in a demand for a free and secret choice of candidates—though it must be admitted that after forty years this stage has not yet been reached in Russia.

Public Health and Education

The People's Republic of China has some impressive accomplishments to its credit in the fields of public health and education. In public health great progress has been made in the control of epidemics, in providing some sort of elementary medical care for the whole population, and in medical education. Epidemics have been brought under control by massive nationwide campaigns for the destruction of such disease carriers as rats and flies. The pitifully small number of qualified doctors and nurses that the Communists found available, and that formerly had been mostly concentrated in the larger cities, was redeployed, and time was rationed out in such a way as to give some kind of medical coverage to the whole population. Crash programs of medical education were instituted—short term courses to give training in simple techniques, and greatly increased stress on a more adequate and full length medical training.

Most interesting of all, the large number of "native doctors" were integrated into the health program. Though without modern scientific training, they did understand the use of some helpful drugs, and they had valuable experience in the diagnosis of disease. When this background of experience had been supplemented by short term courses in a few of the simpler modern techniques, it was felt that the native doctors would provide an indispensable stopgap until a more adequate number of properly trained medical personnel was available. The result of all this has been a rapid rise in the life expectancy of the population.

In education, too, Communist achievements have been impressive. In their tenth anniversary celebrations in 1959 the following figures were released, and they are probably fairly accurate:

	1949 Enrollment	1959 Enrollment
Higher education	130,058	660,000
Secondary "	1,271,342	11,990,000
Primary "	23,683,492	86,400,000

In such a rapid growth, the quality level was certainly lowered, for there were simply not the qualified teachers available. But here, as in the public health program, the Communist government believes that it is a sound practice to sacrifice quality for quantity, that is, it is better for everyone to get some education, even though in the process some educational standards are lowered.

43

Of especial interest is the Communist emphasis upon correlating education with the industrial needs of the nation. Not only is a much higher proportion of education devoted to technical and industrial courses than previously, but also all students, those in "liberal arts" as well as those in the applied sciences, are required to spend a considerable proportion of their time in productive work in factories or fields. According to one widely recognized standard, a student should spend eight months in study, three months in productive labor, and one month in rest every year. Another standard divided the seven days of the week into four and a half days of study, one and a half days of productive labor, and one day of rest.

Political activity has also made great demands upon the student's time. Every political campaign—and the Communist government of China gets all its work done by a constant series of high-pressure campaigns—feels free to call upon the schools to send out their students to take part in parades, or kill rats, or hunt for evidences of corruption, or go around making propaganda speeches. There is no question that these demands have constituted a serious encroachment upon the student's time, though possibly in a few cases the activities themselves have had a certain amount of educational value. As a result of this practical emphasis, there has been little development of work on the graduate level.

The emphasis upon technical training has made it possible for both industry and agriculture to achieve a remarkable advance in the use of laborsaving machinery. While what has aptly been described as the "anthill method"—thousands of coolies trotting back and forth carrying dirt, stones, bricks, and other material—is still a necessary part of every large public work, there is an almost fanatic stress upon the need to mechanize. Every moderate sized city has its electric plant. Chinese-made trucks are beginning to come off the assembly line. Thousands of miles of railroads and automobile roads have been built, and the whole country is being tied together in a postal, telegraph, and airplane network that is daily becoming more comprehensive in its scope.

The People's Republic of China is strongly militaristic. It came to power on the strength of the People's Liberation Army, and that army is kept strong and ready to fight. In 1951 a so-called volunteer force from that army fought the combined United Nations armies in Korea, and forced them back from near the Yalu River to the 38th parallel. As a result China is once again, after hundreds of years of eclipse, coming to be recognized as one of the great and powerful nations of the world. This enhanced prestige gives great satisfaction to Chinese everywhere.

It is apparent from the account above that the People's Republic of China can claim the support of many high-minded and conscientious citizens. There are even many Christian Chinese, and possibly a majority of them, who join in this support, and for reasons that we cannot help but respect: (1) The Communist government has ended the civil war that was ravaging the country and brought peace and stability. (2) It has overcome the ruinous inflation and other economic disorders that had so plagued the country under Nationalist rule. (3) Its positive programs of universal education and health care have appealed to the ethical sense of all, including Christians, and have been a powerful argument on behalf of the Communist claim to care for the common man. (4) There was from the beginning a tremendous patriotic appeal. Communism carefully avoided any appearance of being a foreign ideology and claimed instead to fulfill the legitimate aspirations of all patriotic Chinese. (5) There was no practical alternative to the support of this government. The Nationalist alternative rapidly lost all appeal after the retreat from the mainland, and the only remaining choice was between communism and chaos.

In these conditions the support that the Chinese church has given to the People's Republic of China becomes intelligible, if not justified. Not justified, for some precious values of the human spirit—fundamental human freedoms —have been lost. Because of this, we may well question whether China has not sold its birthright for a mess of pottage.

Steps to Preserve the Church from Destruction

In 1948, as the Communist takeover began to appear more and more inevitable, the whole of the Christian church throughout the country was filled with a sense of uncertainty. Missionaries and Chinese Christian leaders alike found it impossible to predict what would happen to the church in a Communist-controlled China. Many of them worked on the basis of assumptions that now in retrospect seem to have been very naive. It must be remembered, however, that at that time there seemed no sure ground for predicting what a Communist government would do.

Many Americans felt, for example, that China was so dependent on its trade with America that no government, no matter how hostile its ideology, would venture to cut off relations altogether. Therefore, the missionary might be able to continue to serve the Chinese church, though perhaps with some of his activities curtailed. Later events showed that assumption to be completely wrong. Although the American government seemed to be offering a *de facto* recognition by leaving its ambassador, John Leighton Stuart, in Nanking to treat with the new regime, the latter refused from the beginning to regard him as anything more than a private American citizen. The country was sealed off from the outside world, and no missionaries who happened at that time to be at home on furlough were given permission to re-enter the country. The missionaries who were still at their posts were immediately placed under severe travel restrictions. They had been accustomed to travel at will throughout the country, and indeed their work, dealing with and serving a widely scattered church, made it necessary for them to travel over several counties or even over several provinces. But now every foreigner found himself confined to the city of his residence. In that city he could, unless for some reason he was placed under house arrest or imprisoned, move about freely, but he could never leave the city limits without special permission, a permission that in many instances proved almost impossible to obtain.

Even within that narrow territorial limit, the work of the missionary was more and more restricted. Chinese church leaders were told that it was unpatriotic to have aliens, and in particular possibly hostile aliens, as members of the governing boards of schools and hospitals; missionaries should be eased out of such positions as rapidly as possible.

The official attitude toward missionaries was in general frigidly polite up to the time of the entrance of the Chinese "volunteer army" into the fighting in Korea. Then the government's position changed almost overnight. In Nanking, for example, all the church leaders were called by the mayor to a meeting to consider the church contribution to the national war effort. In this meeting the mayor said to them, "We are having more difficulty with you church leaders over this matter than with any other segment of the population, and the reason is that you have daily contacts with enemy aliens and unconsciously absorb their point of view. If you want to be considered as patriotic Chinese citizens, you must resolutely cut off all contact with these enemy aliens."

This changed attitude convinced most of the missionaries still remaining in China that their days of usefulness there were over, and that their continued presence would be a source of embarrassment to their Chinese colleagues. The result was that by the fall of 1950 the trickle of departing missionaries had swollen to a steady stream. By the end of 1951 the exodus was practically complete. Those who were still left in China were either in prison, under house arrest, or for some unexplained reason denied exit permits.

Considering the war psychology that prevailed in the People's Republic, the number of Protestant missionaries sentenced to prison terms on a charge of espionage was comparatively small. Paul Mackensen, a United Lutheran missionary in Tsingtao, was sentenced to five years imprisonment; Dr. and Mrs. Homer V. Bradshaw and Miss Sara Perkins, Presbyterian missionaries in Canton, were in prison until the end of 1955; Olin Stockwell, a Methodist missionary in Chungking, Presbyterian missionary John

Hayes, and a score or more of others were in prison for various shorter terms. There was little physical maltreatment to complain of, though some of the rather numerous Roman Catholic missionaries who were imprisoned seem to have been less fortunate in this respect.

Most of the missionaries who stayed on into the Communist regime received their exit permits soon after requesting them, or perhaps after delays that though exasperating were not very consequential. By early 1951 it can be said that the missionaries were either out of the country or so separated from the work of the church as to be the equivalent of absent. Thus the first objective of the Communist government in regard to the Christian church—to get rid of the missionaries—was accomplished.

Connected with this antimissionary policy was the determination to free the church from all dependence upon foreign funds. At first the government was willing to allow for a period of several years of decreasing foreign assistance to the weaker churches and to various church institutions. But the fighting in Korea brought heightened tensions between America and China, and this resulted, in December, 1950, in a "freezing" order from America forbidding the transfer of American funds to China. China immediately retaliated by prohibiting any organization in China from receiving any aid from abroad, thus precipitating a financial crisis for many of the less favorably situated of the mission institutions.

By these two actions, the separating of the missionaries from all contact with the church and the cutting off of aid from abroad, the government made sure that it would have to deal with a purely Chinese church, and therefore one that would be more susceptible to national pressures.

The Christian Manifesto

Chinese Christian leaders recognized the cataclysmic nature of the changes that were in process sooner than their missionary colleagues. As early as the spring of 1950, a group of Chinese Christian leaders prepared a message to mission boards abroad in which there was this startling paragraph:

From now on, a new political concept, a new philosophy, a new creed, and a new mode of living will be instilled into the masses of the people with a vigor that is hitherto unknown. Much of China's traditional heritage will be rigorously scrutinized and if need be discarded, and many new and far-reaching policies will be put into execution. Likewise, much of Western culture that has been introduced in recent years will be reexamined and shorn of its undesirable elements. Out of this will be born a new China, radically different from the China of old. Compared with the present moment, the change of dynasties in the past four thousand years has little significance; the revolutions of 1911 and 1927 and the war of resistance against Japan are but wavelets in the rapids of time. From such a change there is no turning back, and at such a time a die-hard reaction has no place.

This statement was comparatively noncommittal about the attitude of Christians toward the expected changes, but a later statement, the so-called Christian Manifesto, was more explicit.

The history of the Christian Manifesto is full of interest. It resulted from a visit to Peking by several Shanghai church leaders in May 1950. Y.M. and Y.W. Secretaries Y. T. Wu and Cora Deng, Church of Christ in China General Secretary H. H. Ts'ui, and Lutheran leader Ai Nien-san went to Peking to consult with Premier Chou En-lai on how best to show the church's loyalty to the new regime. In Peking they were joined by several of the northern church leaders, including Methodist Bishop Z. T. Kaung and Yenching University theology professor T. C. Chao. The group succeeded in having three lengthy interviews with Chou En-lai on May 2, 6, and 13. At the last of these three meetings the first draft of the Manifesto, which had been written largely by Y. T. Wu, was presented to the Premier and approved by him.

This first draft met with widespread criticism when it was presented to church leaders in Shanghai. On their insistence, Y. T. Wu consented to a few minor changes. He then took the revision back to Peking and got Chou En-lai's consent for the revised form. Afterwards, when the brethren in Shanghai demanded still more revision and moderation in the language, they were told that no further change could be admitted since this was the official form of the Manifesto as approved by the Premier. The Sheng Kung Hui (Anglican) bishops thereupon withdrew from participation in the statement and issued their own.

In spite of these widespread misgivings, the Manifesto was finally published in July 1950 under the title: "Direction of Endeavor for Chinese Christianity in the Construction of New China." It appeared over the signatures of forty of the outstanding Christian leaders of China, and immediately a campaign was started to give it wider sponsorship. By September it had 1,527 signatures of church leaders, and a year or two later the number of signers had reached 400,000—almost half of the total Protestant membership in the country. For this reason, and also because it constituted a blueprint of future church action, the Manifesto is worth quoting in full:

Protestant Christianity has been introduced to China for more than a hundred and forty years. During this period it has made a not unworthy contribution to Chinese society. Nevertheless, and this was most unfortunate, not long after Christianity's coming to China, imperialism started its activities here; and since the principal groups of missionaries who brought Christianity to China all came themselves from these imperialistic countries, Christianity consciously or unconsciously, directly or indirectly, became related with imperialism. Now that the Chinese revolution has achieved victory, these imperialistic countries will not rest passively content in face of this unprecedented historical fact in China. They will certainly seek to contrive by every means the destruction of what has actually been achieved; they may also make use of Christianity to forward their plot of stirring up internal dissension, and creating reactionary forces in this country. It is our purpose in publishing the following statement to heighten our vigilance against imperialism, to make known the clear political stand of Christians in New China, to hasten the building of a Chinese church whose affairs are managed by the Chinese themselves, and to indicate the responsibilities that should be taken up by Christians throughout the whole country in national reconstruction in New China. We desire to call upon all Christians in the country to exert their best efforts in putting into effect the principles herein presented.

THE TASK IN GENERAL

Christian churches and organizations give thoroughgoing support to the "Common Political Platform," and under the leadership of the government oppose imperialism, feudalism, and bureaucratic capitalism, and take part in the effort to build an independent, democratic, peaceable, unified, prosperous, and powerful New China.

FUNDAMENTAL AIMS

(1) Christian churches and organizations in China should exert their utmost efforts, and employ effective methods, to make people in the churches everywhere recognize clearly the evils that have been wrought in China by imperialism; recognize the fact that in the past imperialism has made use of Christianity; purge imperialistic influences from within Christianity itself; and be vigilant against imperialism, and especially American imperialism, in its plot to use religion in fostering the growth of reactionary forces. At the same time, the churches and organizations should call upon Christians to participate in the movement opposing war and upholding peace, and teach them thoroughly to understand and support the government's policy of agrarian reform.

(2) Christian churches and organizations in China should take effective measures to cultivate a patriotic and democratic spirit among their adherents in general, as well as a psychology of self-respect and self-reliance. The movement for autonomy, self-support, and self-propagation hitherto promoted in the Chinese church has already attained a measure of success. This movement from now onwards should complete its tasks within the shortest possible period. At the same time, self-criticism should be advocated, all forms of Christian activity re-examined

and readjusted, and thoroughgoing austerity measures adopted, so as to achieve the goals of a reformation in the church.

CONCRETE METHODS

(1) All Christian churches and organizations in China that are still relying upon foreign personnel and financial aid should work out concrete plans to realize within the shortest possible time their objective of self-reliance and rejuvenation.

(2) From now onwards, as regards their religious work, Christian churches and organizations should lay emphasis upon a deeper understanding of the nature of Christianity itself, closer fellowship and unity among the various denominations, the cultivation of better leadership personnel, and reform in systems of church organization. As regards their more general work, they should emphasize anti-imperialistic, anti-feudalistic and anti-bureaucratic-capitalistic education, together with such forms of service to the people as productive labor, teaching them to understand the New Era, cultural and recreational activities, literacy education, medical and public health work, and care of children.

The reader will note that in the first paragraph of this Manifesto the charge is made that the whole missionary movement of the past 140 years, though praiseworthy in its original inception, became the puppet of the imperialistic aims of the countries from which the missionaries came. In a later paragraph the United States is specifically mentioned as the front offender in this respect. This singling out of the United States is not the result of a fair and impartial analysis of the history of the past century and a half, but rather a corollary of the Communist line that the United States is the leader of the anticommunist forces.

55

It is true that various colonialist and imperialist pressures were exerted upon China by the countries of the West, and that in some cases these pressures were exerted on behalf of the missionary enterprise. It is also true that some missionaries, after acquiring familiarity with the country of China in their missionary work, took temporary or permanent service under their own government, thus placing at the disposal of that government the intimate knowledge of China that they had gained.

The mission boards themselves were prompt to take advantage of all concessions wrung from an unwilling Chinese government. There was, for example, the immediate missionary occupation of the five treaty ports opened to foreign residence at the end of the Opium War in 1842. But charges that the missionaries were undercover agents of their own governments, or that the mission boards consciously lent themselves to imperialistic designs cannot be substantiated by a fair reading of history. Their currency in China today—and ever since the Manifesto this view is uniformly reflected in all publications coming from mainland China—must be put down as a characteristic exaggeration of nationalistic propaganda due to war or cold war pressures. This is a type of perversion of history from which the West, even within Christian circles, is not wholly free.

The denunciation of the missionary movement increased in intensity in later years, and finally came to an almost complete negation of the rather cautious approval voiced in the second sentence of the Manifesto, namely, that Protestant Christianity has made a "not unworthy contribution to Chinese society." How a Chinese Christian could remain an adherent of a religion that he was picturing as having come to him through such perverted channels is an anomaly not unlike those often found in the history of the West when Christian truth and political expediency have formed an uneasy partnership.

But in 1950 the Manifesto could still acknowledge a "not unworthy contribution," and even secular organs could take a comparatively mild view of the situation. The Shanghai *Ta Kung Pao,* a semi-official newspaper, on October 26, 1950, published an editorial approving of the Manifesto, and saying in part: "Christianity came to China quite recently, and so the number of its adherents is not large. Still, they are quite influential. Since Christianity from its beginning brought with it many cultural and scientific agencies, such as hospitals, schools, and libraries, so the cultural level of Chinese Christians is on the whole well above the average of the country and their activities in society are numerous."

Another point that may impress the Western reader of this Manifesto is the standard repetition of the phrase "Christian churches and organizations." The use of this phrase is an indication of the importance in the Christian enterprise in China of its schools, hospitals, and other organizations. They equaled or in some places even overshadowed the significance of the church itself.

At the time this Manifesto was published, the mission boards were still operating in China, a fair proportion of the missionaries were still on the field, and the schools and hospitals were still in the hands of the church. This situation changed radically in the period immediately ensuing when all educational and welfare activities were declared to be properly the function of the state. As a result all the schools, hospitals, and orphanages were taken over by the government, always without any compensation to the church for the millions of dollars worth of property thus confiscated. The only organizations left to the church were the theological and Bible schools, the Bible House, and similar Christian publishing agencies. The continued existence of these organizations, however, might well have seemed very doubtful, for they had always relied heavily upon foreign support, which, as we have seen, was cut off completely in December, 1950. That even such a limited number of agencies has been able to continue at all to the present day was only due to a drastic reduction in the scope of the activities to not more than one-tenth of what they had been before 1950. This reduction freed about nine-tenths of their property holdings for rental, thus providing an income by which they have been able to maintain the remaining tenth.

The Three Self Reform Movement

To carry through the complete reorientation of Christian thought outlined above, it was necessary to have a new church organization, and this was provided by what is now called the Three Self Reform Movement. The term "Three Self" was intended to emphasize the newly gained independence of the church from all foreign control, and is a characteristic Chinese abbreviation of "self-support, self-government, and self-propagation."

This ideal for the church of self-support, self-government, and self-propagation had long been pushed by missionaries and mission boards, and great progress had been made towards its implementation in the preceding half century. But in the very nature of the case, the ideal could never be completely realized as long as large sums of money for the furtherance of church work continued to come from abroad. Even if no other strings were attached to the gifts, it still would often happen that the grants would be made to projects that the Western church considered important rather than to projects that the Chinese church would have preferred. And wherever the missionaries were of a "bossy" nature, there was always a great temptation to use the power of the purse strings to determine church policy. Now, under governmental direction, this interdenominational church agency was to proclaim the complete independence of the Chinese church from all foreign control and vigorously attack all thought and action within the church that was sympathetic to the older missionary regime.

Other religious groups submitted to a similar regimentation. In the Roman Catholic Church, the Catholic Patriotic Association was organized. Though firmly in the saddle since 1958, it had more difficulty in establishing itself as Catholic spokesman than the Three Self Movement had in Protestant circles. There are two reasons for this. First, the Roman Catholic Church had put itself on record as anticommunist in a much more thoroughgoing way than Prot-

estant churches had. Secondly, loyalty to a foreign author-
ity, the Pope, was an integral part of the Catholic faith,
while there was nothing in Protestant teaching that laid
down such a challenge to the resurgent nationalism of the
New China. It required the wholesale imprisonment of both
foreign and Chinese bishops and priests, and the intervention of the police to place control of church property in
the hands of "patriotic" Catholics, before the Catholic Patriotic Association could make headway within the church.

Buddhism and Islam were similarly regimented under
newly created national organizations. Taoism was at first
too amorphous to be able to create such an organization
for itself, and so for several years it labored under the
disadvantage of being an illegitimate and unauthorized religion. It has now, however, fulfilled the requirement of a
sort of national organization, and so has been granted a
limited recognition—limited because Taoism teems with
secret societies, and these are anathema to the Communists.

First steps were taken toward the formation of the Three
Self Reform Movement for Protestant churches in 1950,
at the time when the Manifesto was promulgated. But a
formally recognized organization did not come into existence until the spring of 1951. At that time (April 16-21) the
Religious Affairs Bureau of the government brought to
Peking 151 Protestant leaders from all over the country for
what was officially known as a "Conference on Dealing
with Christian Institutions Formerly Receiving American
Aid." Here was set up an organization with the cumber-
some name of "Preparatory Committee of the China Chris-

tian (Resist America Help Korea) Three Self Reform Movement Committee." The words in parenthesis were put in at this time because the Korean War was still going on. Later they were dropped.

Y. T. Wu

The key figure in this whole development was a Y.M.C.A. secretary by the name of Y. T. Wu (Wu Yao-tsung). Mr. Wu was born in Canton in 1893. He came from a non-Christian family and was converted to Christianity when he was a student in Customs College, Peking. In 1924 and again in 1937 he studied at Union Theological Seminary in New York City, and in the later period was much influenced by the teaching of Harry Ward and Reinhold Niebuhr. He was ordained in the Congregational Church in June, 1920.

Throughout his career as a Y.M.C.A. secretary, Wu has always worked for the realization in society of what he considered to be Christian ideals. In the early twenties he was the organizer of the China branch of the Fellowship of Reconciliation, to which he gave the expressive name of Love Only Society, that is, a society of those who have resolved to settle all questions by the use of love alone. He served as executive secretary of the Student Division of the national Y.M.C.A., 1929-32, and then became national literature secretary of the Association Press, in which capacity he sponsored the publication in Chinese of many important and serious works on the Christian religion, including translations of such works as Lyman's *Meaning and*

Truth of Religion and Goodspeed's *Story of the Bible.* In the period following the Second World War his interest in the social gospel increased, and he had a translation of one of Walter Rauschenbusch's works ready for publication when the Communists took over. Of course, the government would not allow the discussion of important social questions from the standpoint of Christianity rather than that of communism, so the book was never offered for sale.

In 1949 he was drawn into the Communist sponsored peace movement and attended the peace conferences in Prague and Paris. He had previously abandoned the Fellowship of Reconciliation ideal of pacifism, and in a magazine article in 1952 says of it, "It was a beautiful dream. But now thirty years later I have completely awakened from this dream. I have not abandoned my hopes for world peace, but now I know that peace will never be achieved by indulging in idle fantasies, but only through struggle."

Immediately upon his return to China from Prague and Paris, Mr. Wu threw himself into the task of preparing the church to accept the new regime. It seems clear that he was motivated by an honest conviction of the value of communism, a sincere love for the church, and a desire to save it from destruction. Approval cannot be given to all that he has done through the Three Self Movement. He has allowed the church to become a "captive church," doing nothing but parrot the Communist line. But he undoubtedly felt that this was the only alternative to complete destruction. He was misled by a too optimistic expectation of tolerance of religion from the Communist government and by a failure to appreciate the depth of meaning in Tertullian's famous dictum that "The blood of the martyrs is the seed of the church."

He was also motivated by a view of history that he had elaborated on the basis of Communist doctrine. According to the latter, world history has proceeded from original primitive communism through the well-marked stages of slavery, feudalism, and capitalism to the present period when socialism is destined to take the place of capitalism. Accepting this philosophy of history, Mr. Wu links the Roman Catholic Church with feudalism and the Protestant church with capitalism. He believes that with the introduction of socialism as great a reformation will be required in church life as took place under Luther and Calvin. It is the duty of the Three Self Movement to carry this reformation through for the church in China. This view he outlined in a series of articles published in the Shanghai newspaper *Ta Kung Pao* in July, 1949.

As organizer of the Three Self Movement Committee he became its chairman, and has directed its activities in all the years since. He was therefore directly responsible for one of the most questionable chapters in the history of the Chinese church, namely, the denunciation movement.

The Denunciation Movement

The denunciation movement began in April, 1951, in Peking, with the Conference of 151 (cf. p. 60) establishing the pattern for the denunciation meetings. Previously there had been sporadic attacks on various individuals, but now under the active direction of Communist government officials, several key figures in the Protestant church were chosen for attack. The missionaries were Southern Presbyterian Frank W. Price and Canton Y.M.C.A. Secretary Edward Lockwood. The Chinese church leaders attacked were Methodist Bishop W. Y. Ch'en, Sheng Kung Hui Bishop Y. Y. Tsü, Y. M. C. A. Secretary S. C. Leung, and roving evangelist Ku Jen-en. Lockwood, Tsü, and Leung were out of the country, so the denunciation of them was an empty gesture. Ch'en and Ku had already been put in prison, where the former served a five year term. The latter was never heard from again. Why Dr. Price, who was living in Shanghai at the time, was not arrested is one of the mysteries of this period. He told me recently that for months he had a small suitcase packed ready to take with him if the police should call to escort him to jail. During this period he frequently heard directed mob slogans demanding his death broadcast over the radio.

One of the most diabolical features of the whole denunciation program was the demand by the government that the denunciation speeches be made by those who had been the victim's closest friends and associates. Thus Dr. Price's accusers in the April meeting in Peking were his associate in the secretariat of the Church of Christ in China, the Rev. H. H. Ts'ui; one of his closest friends from the long period of his residence in Nanking, Dr. Luther Shao; and an associate in student work, Miss Shih Ju-chang of the Y.W.C.A. Bishop W. Y. Ch'en's prime accuser was his colleague, Bishop Z. T. Kaung, Y.M.C.A. Secretary S. C.

Leung was accused by his colleague, Kiang Wen-han, and Sheng Kung Hui Bishop Y. Y. Tsü by the presiding bishop of that church, Bishop Robin Ch'en. The purpose of this requirement was to make the break with the former order of things as complete as possible, on the sound psychological theory that once you have denounced a former friend publicly your mind will automatically go on looking for further evidence to justify this betrayal of friendship.

To us in the West, it seems almost inconceivable that good Christians could be induced to denounce in this heartless way those who had been their closest friends and associates. But it must be remembered that it was a time when nationalistic feeling was running high, and the demand was put on a patriotic basis. You must not, they were told, allow private sentiment to stand in the way of your patriotic duty. The conflict in your mind is between public duty and private feeling, and of these two, it is the former that should have priority.

Both H. H. Ts'ui and Luther Shao have made poignant statements of how they wrestled in agony over this conflict between public duty and private feeling, noting how the final resolution of the conflict in the fulfilling of their public duty brought them peace and satisfaction.

Long suppressed resentments against the semi-foreign aspects of church life and a desire to show that Christians were not alienated from the main stream of Chinese culture also played their part in this demonstration.

There is one caution, however, that is to be kept in mind in regard to all denunciation speeches—and this applies to the confession articles reported in Chapter 5 as well—namely, that we cannot be at all sure that the published form of these speeches is what the speakers really said or thought. It has always been standard Communist practice to insist on the right of revision of all such speeches and articles, and sometimes after a speech has been delivered in a public meeting the published form in the newspapers is made harsher still. A vivid description of Mary Liu's experience with Communist editing of what she said is given in Edward Hunter's book *The Story of Mary Liu.* Expressions that she would not have used were written into her speech, and then she did not dare to omit them. After the speech was given, the form of it as released for publication was still more extreme. It is quite possible, therefore, that the statements made below do not so much represent what Chinese Christian leaders said as what the Communist controlled press represented them as saying. Still, the gist of these articles must have been at least reluctantly agreed to by the purported writer.

The general pattern of these denunciation speeches is as follows: First, a general statement of denunciation, usually couched in very strong, not to say violent language; then a list of particulars to substantiate the accusation; and finally a demand that the government mete out proper punishment for such betrayal of the Chinese people. Strangely enough, the bill of particulars often seems like a flat anticlimax after the strong language of the opening statement, for usually nothing can be adduced that would not have seemed a perfectly normal action in the period before 1949. This fact makes the final demand for punishment often seem forced and unreal.

For example, Bishop Kaung's speech is entitled "I Denounce That Christian Reprobate W. Y. Ch'en," and he begins, "Today I arise with extreme indignation and shame to denounce that Christian reprobate W. Y. Ch'en, who, hidden within the Methodist Church, has been a willing tool of American imperialism and bandit Chiang Kai-shek, and has worked against the people and against the revolution." To justify these words against a brother bishop he lists three particulars: 1. W. Y. Ch'en was a speaker much in demand at meetings of the Nationalist party's Youth Corps. 2. He co-operated with Madame Chiang in pushing the New Life Movement, a movement designed to rehabilitate some of the old Confucian virtues. 3. In visits to England and America in the years 1943-1948 he often spoke on behalf of the Nationalist government. Finally, he thanks the Communists for having already arrested Bishop Ch'en, and asks that they punish him severely according to law. "I must also make a deep criticism of myself, and I call upon all Methodists to unite in casting out of the church such reprobates. I am determined to put public duty above private feeling in reorganizing our church, and will cleanse the church of all reprobates like W. Y. Ch'en, whether they be few or many [the record reports here "Great Applause"], so that the Methodist Church may become a pure Methodist Church of the Chinese people, and under the direction of the government unitedly and positively participate in the Resist America Help Korea Movement as well as all other anti-imperialistic movements, and thus help to build the New China."

The 151 delegates to the Peking Conference immediately proceeded upon their return home to arrange similar denunciation meetings. They were warned, however, not to do it on their own, but to work under the direction and with the assistance of the local government authorities. That would mean that the persons to be accused would in most cases be chosen by the government rather than by the church leaders, and then it would be the duty of the church to find the necessary accusing data.

Both missionaries and Chinese church leaders were included among the objects of denunciation. But in this early period special attention was paid to the former, in order to hasten the process of completely weaning the church away from its affection for its former spiritual directors. The denunciation, therefore, was not confined to those missionaries who were still on the field, but included also those who had already returned to their homes and were thus beyond the range of punitive action. It even extended to many of the great names of past generations.

In this connection any Chinese who in any public way had expressed appreciation for the work of the missionaries was obliged to accuse himself and recant his former statements. For example, the scholar Wang Chih-hsin—at an earlier time a professor in the University of Shanghai, but at this time teaching in Nanking Theological Seminary —had written a history of the Protestant church in China, and this book naturally had a good many appreciative things to say about the missionaries. For this he had to write an article humbly admitting his mistakes, withdraw the book from circulation, and write a new history of the church that should embody the now orthodox view of mission activities.

Sheng Kung Hui Bishop Michael Chang of Foochow had a similar experience. Late in 1950 the Foochow Anglican diocese had celebrated one hundred years of existence, and Bishop Chang had praised many of his missionary predecessors in a public address and in a pastoral letter to the churches of his diocese. Six months later he humbly admitted his mistake in an address that was recorded as follows in *Tien Feng*, a Christian magazine published in Shanghai:

This evening I am filled with indignation and shame as I stand here to make a general denunciation of the imperialism that has used the Sheng Kung Hui in Fukien for its aggression against China. At the same time I am making an examination of my own life.

A half year ago when we celebrated our centennial, although the missionaries had all left, still our minds were so filled with reverence and respect for the missionaries that we mistakenly ascribed the results of one hundred years of labor to their devotion. We thought them all good and kind, and felt that we should thank them for their favors. This unprincipled fawning upon foreigners is plainly to be seen in the address I gave at that time and in the pastoral letter I sent to my diocese. I did not then have sufficient trust in the People's Republic, or in their policy of freedom of religious belief. At that time, six months ago, Foochow had already been liberated for more than a year, but my thinking was still confused. As I examine it now

I see that it was full of imperialist poison. I thank the People's Republic for giving me many opportunities to attend many meetings for patriotic study. In June our church had a denunciation movement that still further awakened me, and led me to see that all I had previously said and done was wrong. This evening I want to take a fresh point of view and re-evaluate our one hundred years of history and the place of missionaries in that history. I will no longer call our patriots bandits who persecute the church, nor will I praise imperialist elements as devout and holy missionaries. I fully realize that the Christianity preached by the missionaries, since they came from an imperialist country, had had its original purity corrupted by the addition of many imperialist and even anti-Christian thoughts. . . .

Bishop Chang then went on to give a fresh evaluation of that one hundred years of history, singling out John R. Wolfe, W. P. W. Williams, and David Paton as typical imperialists of the periods 1850-1900, 1901-1944, and 1945-1950, respectively. By means of this confession, he was able to blunt the edge of the attack upon him, but he was so unnerved by the experience that he retired in poor health to Shanghai, leaving the work of the diocese to his two suffragan bishops. Several years later, however, he was able to return to Foochow and presumably resumed his episcopal responsibilities.

It is to be noted that denunciation and personal confession went hand-in-hand in both of the speeches reported above. In the reorientation of thought that was now demanded of everyone (for the process here described as going on in Christian circles was likewise going on in all other circles of society), it was necessary that all the imperialistic and individualistic influences that had helped to shape each person's life be brought to light, confessed, and denounced. The public denunciation of these influences, and of the persons through whom they had been purveyed, was therefore looked upon as a necessary proof that the personal confession that had been made was sincere, and that the reorientation of thought had actually taken place.

The havoc that all this created in personal relations can easily be imagined. Was the thinking of those persons you considered your best friends to the left or to the right of yours? If to the left, were they even now preparing to denounce you as a reactionary? If to the right, is it your duty to denounce them? If you don't denounce them, will you get in trouble yourself? In countless breasts fear and suspicion took the place of friendly confidence; cautious silence, the place of frank discussion.

Thus by the end of 1951, the government had succeeded in isolating the Protestant church in China from all relationship with the churches of the free world: the missionaries were gone or immobilized, no more money was coming from mission boards, and the church was embarked on a program of denouncing all its former connections with the West. Theoretically it was admitted that some missionaries and some mission activity had been beneficial to China, but it was dangerous to reduce this generality to specifics, and so no attempt was made to distinguish between the sheep and the goats of the missionary enterprise. From this time on any reference to a former missionary is uniformly qualified by the invidious adjective "imperialist."

This Communist success had been brought about by the co-operation of the Three Self Reform Movement. As a result the latter has often been denounced out of hand in the West as a fundamental betrayal of Christian principles. China Inland Mission missionary Leslie Lyall in his book *Come Wind, Come Weather* writes of the Manifesto in a chapter entitled "The Manifesto of Betrayal." This is too harsh and ungenerous a judgment on fellow Christians. It is true that the Three Self leaders co-operated with the Communist government to a degree that seems excessive. But the old Chinese proverb, "They slept in the same bed, but they dreamed different dreams," is worth recalling here. The government sought to achieve the complete socialization of the country, and for that purpose they felt that they must subjugate the church. The Three Self leaders, on the other hand, had the purpose of preserving the church from destruction. They felt that the only way to achieve this purpose was to show the government that the church would not be an obstruction in the march toward the Marxist goal. Both sides have in a measure achieved their respective purposes. The church still exists, though at the cost of many sacrifices and questionable compromises.

In 1954 Y. T. Wu published a series of essays in a church magazine in Shanghai with the subject Freedom Through Truth. In one of these he speaks to discouraged Christians in words that should suffice to dispel any doubts of the sincerity of his Christian faith. He said: "Since Liberation we frequently hear Christians asking, 'Has Christianity any future?' That is a strange question to be upon the lips of a

Christian. What has happened to his faith? Does he believe that the eternal God who made heaven and earth exists today and will not exist tomorrow? Has he forgotten that the Christ whose life was full of mercy and truth is the same yesterday, today, and forever? Does he believe that the Holy Spirit who has hitherto enlightened and guided his heart will now suddenly stop working? Not so. The eternal Triune God does not change with the times. It is not the faithfulness of God that we need to be concerned about, but our own faithfulness. If we have deeds to match our faith, if we make an effective witness for Jesus Christ, then all our anxieties will be found to have been needless."

Training in Communist Theory

The separation from the old order as described in Chapter 4 was a negative process. The Communists had also a positive program of training in the new order. As noted in Chapter 3, the whole population was subjected to a systematic indoctrination in Communist thinking. By far the larger part of this indoctrination was carried on through weekly (or oftener) lectures and discussions. All those who were in a position to influence the thinking of others, such as teachers and preachers, had to take part in more extended study classes. There was no standard length of time for these classes—some lasted two weeks, and some went on for three or four months. Students involved in the longer indoctrination sessions had to get leaves of absence from the work they were doing and give themselves completely to study. Christian preachers were usually organized into study classes by themselves, and the Three Self Reform Movement took joint responsibility with the Religious Affairs Bureau of the gov-

ernment for the direction of the classes and the retraining
of the group.

Indoctrination of Preachers

The first extended indoctrination class for preachers was
held in Shanghai in the fall of 1953. Ninety-nine students
were enrolled, eighty-one men and eighteen women. Fifty-
three of them were ordained pastors, and the rest were un-
ordained workers of various sorts. Their ages covered a
wide range: seven were under thirty and one was over
seventy years old. The class began on August 20 and ran
through to November 16. The day's work began with a
half hour devotional period, and the students organized
their own choir that contributed regularly to the program
of this period. The rest of the day was more secular in
character. Nine Communists were appointed by the Religious Affairs Bureau to lecture and lead discussions, but
some of the "progressive" Christian leaders of Shanghai
were also on the staff. The general subjects of discussion
and study ran through the following five stages:

1. Purpose of this study class and the correct attitude toward
   study
2. The greatness and lovableness of our country
   a. Contrast of the Old and the New Chinas
   b. The great accomplishments and prospects of the new
      China
   c. How the New China came into being
3. The nature of imperialism: how it has used the churches
   a. The nature of imperialism

75

The climax of the whole course lay in the personal and autobiographical review essay. In this the student was expected to review his whole past life, show how he had been used by the missionaries for the purposes of cultural aggression, analyze the changes that had taken place in his thinking as a result of the study course, and conclude with an expression of complete identification with the purposes and plans of the new China.

Shen Yi-fan, son of the Anglican Bishop T. K. Shen, was one of these students. His concluding essay was considered one of the best, and it was published in *Tien Feng* magazine. He begins by saying that when he started the course he thought that all this anti-imperialist talk was old stuff; he wouldn't learn much if they continued to harp on that theme. But he found himself forced to re-examine his attitude, and his smugness was shattered.

First, the meaning of patriotism has been made clear to him now. When the Communists came to power he had been prevented from going to England or America to study, and because of this frustration of his individualistic ambitions, he wrote, he hated the Communist party. When the Korean fighting broke out he had hoped the Communists would be overthrown. But now he realizes that he and the mother country (note the unconscious shift from Communist party to mother country) are "of one flesh and blood." He had also thought of the Civil War as just a struggle for power between the Nationalist party and the Communist party. He thought that the Nationalist party was bad, but the Communist party was worse. When members of the latter were put to death by the Nationalists he thought then that they were just getting what was coming to them. Now he sees that they were unselfish martyrs dying for a noble cause. From all of this he learned that love and hate must go together, like the palm and the back of one's hand. The universal love that he had learned from the imperialist missionaries was an "unprincipled love," and so he used to say, "Yes, love China, but why hate America?"

In regard to imperialist aggression, Shen wrote, he learned that it was not just the violent ambition of a few men in the capitalist camp, but that it was the logical result of the capitalist system. He also learned to distinguish between cultural aggression and cultural interchange. The first is bad and the latter good. Formerly he had looked upon cultural aggression as good because he had been getting numerous personal favors through its representatives. He learned here that he must not let gratitude for personal favors warp his judgment of what is evil.

The "reformism" that the missionaries taught had entered deeply into his thinking, so much so that he would even make applications of it before they were suggested to him by his imperialist teachers. Here Mr. Shen gave an example of how he had preached a sermon once on the text about our righteousness exceeding that of the scribes and Pharisees, using the scribes and Pharisees as symbolizing the Communist party. This identification, he said, was never suggested to him in his theology textbooks or by any missionary, but came naturally from the warped thinking of his own mind.

In regard to the message that the church preaches, he used to think that in order to make the church indigenous, all that was necessary was to give the church's liturgy, music, and art a Chinese coloring. Now he sees that the adaptation of the church's message to the new age does not consist in merely adding a few political slogans to its former preaching. The church must first get rid of all imperialist poison from its thinking and learn the pure truth of Christianity from the Bible, then what it preaches will of itself naturally harmonize with many of the truths of this new age. "Until this study I thought that participation in the Three Self Movement was just the price we Christians had to pay for tolerance by the Communist government, so I was only a passive participant. Now I realize that it is necessary to purify the church in this way, in order to oppose imperialism and implement our patriotism. Only the Three Self Movement will close the gap between the people and the church, only the Three Self Movement can break the shackles that have bound the Christian church in China and thus allow the church to make known its pure truth and inner vitality. From now on I will actively and positively participate in this movement, and work for a real Chinese church."

Finally, Shen Yi-fan pays tribute to the government's religious policy of tolerance, which he now believes to be sincere and in accordance with Communist philosophy, and charges the missionaries with having poisoned the minds of Chinese Christians against communism by playing upon the atheism theme.

In this essay there are two points especially worthy of note. First, in spite of the strong procommunist and anti-American tone that pervades the whole essay, Mr. Shen remains a Christian, and in fact is even convinced that now he has grasped the pure truth of Christianity in a way that was impossible to him earlier. It is easy for us here in the West to consider that any one who takes a procommunist stand is turning his back on Christianity. It is possible that Mr. Shen's position is not logical, but nevertheless he holds it, and it may well be questioned whether this position is any more illogical than the tendency of some in the West to associate capitalism with Christianity.

Second, the teaching he received in this study class was clearly a very cleverly compounded amalgam of patriotism and Communist doctrine. Much of what he says simply reflects the awakening of a legitimate patriotic sentiment. The one bit of Communist thinking that he laid hold on in this course was the thought that the capitalist system naturally tends toward aggression. This is a point that is most difficult to refute in view of the history of the past two or three centuries, although it is equally or even more true that the Communist system also tends toward aggression. The one serious blunder that he makes is the naive assumption that once all imperialist poison has been purged from Christian thinking, the pure truth of the Bible will naturally harmonize with much of Communist teaching.

Indoctrination of Educators

Another notable example of a confession essay at the end of an indoctrination course is that of Helen Djang, who had been dean of studies at Ginling College, the Christian college for women in Nanking. As a university professor she had not been included with the church workers, but had studied in what was known as the East China Institute of Political Studies for University Teachers. For this purpose she had taken one semester's leave of absence from her teaching and spent three months in the fall of 1951 at the Institute.

Helen Djang's self-analysis naturally differs greatly from that of Mr. Shen. The point of greatest emphasis in her account is the idea that all mission education, both that which she had received as a student and that which she had dispensed as an educator, had been "comprador education." The word comprador is common in the Far East to denote a native agent of a foreign commercial concern. Her meaning, therefore, is that all the education in which missionaries had been engaged was not for the benefit of the Chinese people, but rather for the benefit of the Western nations. This point she never really proves, but seeks to establish by a sort of "guilt by association" logic. She was apparently so overawed by the whole Communist apparatus of the Institute that she developed a guilt complex, and this led her to make a blanket denunciation of all the foreign influences that had come into her life. But here again, as with Mr. Shen, there is no thought of renouncing her Christian faith, but only of renouncing a foreign influence that she now looks upon as imperialist aggression.

Y. T. Wu's Intellectual Pilgrimage

In these conversions and confessions, Chinese Christians were but following the example of those who were now their leaders. The chairman of the Three Self Reform Movement, Y. T. Wu, had not needed to wait for the impetus of one of these study classes to get his Christian thinking oriented toward Communist doctrine. He had already gone through that process by the time the Communists came to power. Mr. Wu described the progress of his views in the July 7, 1951, issue of the magazine *Tien Feng*. The article, "How the Communist Party Has Educated Me," is so significant that it is worth quoting in full.

HOW THE COMMUNIST PARTY HAS EDUCATED ME

The historical accomplishments and service to the Chinese people of the Chinese Communist party during the past thirty years are incalculable, and impossible to express fully in words. It is due solely to the Chinese Communist party that the Chinese people today can stand erect, receive these blessings and have such a bright outlook for the future.

In the early period—more than twenty years ago—I was anti-

81

communist. At that time I was student secretary in the Peking Y. M. C. A., and whenever I met a student with leftist tendencies I would use Christian teaching to try to correct his "mistaken" thoughts. But the cannon shots of September 18 [1931] awakened me. The development of the movement for saving the nation made me gradually drop my prejudices against the Communist party. In Shanghai I joined the Save the Nation party, where I was indirectly influenced by the Communist party, and I began to realize that Communist thinking and the Communist road of struggle were the only way to save China. Also in the period just before, during, and after the Second World War my reading of such works as those of Lu Hsun and of such magazines as *Chinese Life* and *World Intelligence*, as well as my own experience in opposing Japan, which led me to oppose Chiang Kai-shek and America, all helped me to understand the Communist party better. And now today, after only a little more than a year since Liberation, I have seen with my own eyes the great accomplishments of the Communist party in the construction of the New China, and this not only greatly increases my faith in and admiration of the Communist party, but also leads me to express on behalf of the Chinese people and myself an unbounded affection for the party. Now I want to make a brief report on how the Chinese Communist party has educated me during the past ten to twenty years.

First, it has taught me the true meaning of the verse, "Love your enemies." Not long after I became a Christian, I was influenced by a British Quaker to become a pacifist, that is, to believe that on the basis of Christ's teaching to love our enemies we should oppose all military action. At that time I greatly admired Gandhi and Tolstoi. But the Japanese aggression against China and the Chinese declaration of war on July 7 [1937] unsettled my pacifist ideas. I came to realize that I had misunderstood Christ's teaching: To love your enemies does not mean to condone wrong, the method of persuasion is not enough; on the contrary, one best loves one's enemies by attacking all wrong. Thus I realized that it was the Communists who truly love their enemies, for they on the one hand resolutely carried on war, and on the other treated their Japanese prisoners with kindness and tried to help the Japanese people obtain democratic freedom. Now I am no longer a pacifist, rather I recognize the teaching of pacifism as an imperialist opiate to keep oppressed peoples quiet. It is only by a proper combination of patriotism and internationalism that we can truly love our enemies.

Second, the Communist party helped me to recognize the true face of imperialism, and to see that the most pressing problem today for China, as indeed for the whole world, is how to destroy imperialism and set up peoples' governments. Imperialism really is the devil that Christians talk about. For the sake of a few, it carries on aggression against the whole world, using open war and undercover plots to kill and enslave millions of people. It is the world's deadliest enemy and must be destroyed before the people of the world can obtain true peace, freedom, and prosperity. Formerly I did not understand the international situation well, and considered that all nations were by nature selfish, and that on the international stage there were no such things as right and wrong, justice and injustice. Now from my understanding of imperialism I have gotten a key to the international problem. Now I know that capitalism is an oppressive system that must necessarily produce many domestic and international contradictions and threaten world peace; it is communism, and the socialism and new democracy that form the foundation of communism, that constitute the world's only road to safety.

Third, the Communist party enabled me to understand the true meaning of revolution. Even before I had become a Christian I had already been deeply influenced by those two agents of American imperialism, John R. Mott and Sherwood Eddy.

Mott was for several tens of years the chief agent in spreading American imperialism throughout the world through Christianity. Eddy took the slogan of "reform" and preached the social gospel; he was the American traveling evangelist to the youth of the world. The gospel that they preached was that "character" can save the nation. The Chinese government was sunk in darkness and corruption; to save China we must have men of character, and Christianity is the most effective faith for producing character—this was their theory. Mott and Eddy were two of the most important men in the American Y.M.C.A., and much of the work of the Chinese Y.M.C.A. was based upon the theory that they preached. It proclaimed a fourfold ideal—ethical, scientific, physical, and social—and in its program of religious cultivation, service to workers and farmers, and strength through recreation, its main purpose was the development of "character." But the Communist revolutionary theory led me to see that all of this was but for the purpose of upholding the old society and adorning its walls; at best it was but embroidery upon the old society for the sake of the rich and leisure class. This program could not change the basis of society, it could not bring prosperity to the people as a whole. On the contrary, it drugged the people and sapped their revolutionary strength; it was a preparatory step for imperialistic aggression, and even directly assisted that aggression, so that fundamentally it was a force for reaction. It was Communist influence that changed me from a reformist to a revolutionist. In 1948, on the eve of Liberation, Eddy came to Shanghai for the last time, and in one of his addresses said that Syngman Rhee and MacArthur were two great Christian leaders. When Eddy said this he condemned himself in the eyes of all Chinese Christians as one who committed the sin of using Christianity to further aggression. From this I came to see more clearly the hypocritical nature of American missionaries in general.

Fourth, the Communist party made me understand the true

position of the proletariat. I had formerly thought that since all Christians are children of God they must be all members of one big family, and this was what Christians meant by the word "fellowship," or in more recent terminology by the "ecumenical" nature of Christianity. Accordingly, Christianity is above class and should not encourage class warfare. But the Communist party showed me that the whole of organized Christianity has a class nature. Its claim to be above class is false, and the proletarian standpoint is the only correct one. According to the historical understanding of materialism, the culture of a given period is only the ideology of that society. Christianity is inseparable from culture, and so it is possible for the Christianity of one age to change its nature completely and become a tool of cultural and political aggression, and for Christians themselves on behalf of their own personal interests to throw themselves into the political struggle. As a matter of fact, the larger part of Christendom today is already completely controlled by the capitalist class and by imperialist elements, and has become a tool for their aggression and an enemy of the proletariat. In this understanding the so-called ecumenical nature of Christianity is a deceit, and the so-called fellowship impossible of attainment. On the contrary, it is the duty of Christians to take with non-Christians the standpoint of the proletariat, that is, the standpoint of the people, to oppose exploitation, oppression, and aggression, and work for the true freedom and equality of all the people of the world. If we stand firmly upon this platform, we shall not confuse friend and enemy, or thief and father, and will always see clearly the true purpose of our struggle.

Fifth, the Communist party has shown me the true relation between theory and practice, between faith and deeds. Christianity teaches universal love, and looks for the coming of the kingdom of heaven. When I became a Christian I took this high ideal to heart, but as to how it was to be realized I did not concern myself. Now the Communist party has shattered my empty dreams and made me realize that practice and theory go together. The Communist party not only enlightened my mind but trained me in action. Their action is always according to a system of severe logic, not a mechanical and outward logic but a living and dialectical logic. They use theory to direct practice, and then from the practice get experience by which they improve the theory. The fact that the Chinese Communist party was able, in the short space of thirty years, to become the leader of the Chinese people and complete its revolutionary task in this ancient land, is due to their ability to use this tool of the combination of theory and practice. The so-called scholars of imperialistic Christianity, such as Reinhold Niebuhr in America, have brought forward ingenious theological theories to discredit this Communist point of superiority and to spread anticommunist and anti-Soviet poison. They say: According to fundamental Christian teaching, all men are sinners, and only God is truly good. But if all men are sinners, then every institution of man, including communism, is also sinful. These European and American "scholars" would have us look for an empty ideal, and lay aside the question of its practical realization, while at the same time using this ideal to attack communism. Actually their "ideal" is only a smoke screen. They are not really asking us to seek for an ideal but rather just to uphold the present order—the capitalist and imperialist system that "eats men." This confused theological thinking has deceived millions of well-intentioned Christians, and for a short time influenced my thinking as well. But now the development of world-wide revolutionary strength has disproved this whole theory and has proved the Communist theory to be correct.

During the past ten or fifteen years this education that I have received from the Communist party has had a decisive effect upon my life, and the party is still teaching me. During this time Communist influence has forced me to carry through a long and painful mental struggle. I have been misunderstood, criticized, and attacked by many Christians. Because of this change in my social thinking there has been a very evident change in my theological stand, and as a result I have been condemned as a "leftist" or even as a "heretic." Today, under the direction of the Communist party, all of China has been liberated, the Chinese Christian revolutionary movement is spreading throughout the country, and the thinking of many Christians has already undergone a fundamental change. Much that yesterday was impossible and wrong has become today possible and right. If the "miracles" that Christianity believes in are true, then the fact that the Chinese Communist party in the short space of thirty years has enabled the Chinese people, exploited and oppressed for thousands of years, to stand upon their feet, and at the same time enabled the Chinese Christian church to throw off the shackles of imperialism, is a miracle of a sort heretofore unheard of.

Under the leadership of the Communist party, the future of the New China is bright and glorious, and it is not to be doubted that under the direction of world-wide communism, imperialism will be overthrown and destroyed and the world-wide revolution will be victorious. For all of this I want to express my gratitude to the Chinese Communist party, and congratulate them on the occasion of this the thirtieth anniversary of their founding. At the same time I extend hearty greetings to the Communist parties of other nations.

Rethinking Christian Doctrine

The third of the Reform Movement's three Self's—self-propagation—involved not only taking responsibility for the church's evangelization program but still more a rethinking of the church's message. In this rethinking the interpretation of the uncompromising Christian demand to "love your enemies" has occasioned the most difficulty. Here in the West we have similar difficulty in obeying this command, but we resolve the dilemma by simply disregarding the command; whereas, Chinese Christians have tried to rationalize their limitation of its scope. Besides the reference to this question in both Mr. Shen's and Mr. Wu's articles, there have been literally dozens of articles in the *Tien Feng* magazine in which the authors have tried to harmonize this teaching with the campaigns of hate and denunciation in which they have been involved. One favorite approach is to cite Jesus' condemnation of the scribes and Pharisees and his cleansing of the temple to show that the teaching of love does not mean a spineless acquiescence in evil practices. The thunderings of the Old Testament prophets are also occasionally echoed. The practice of love, it is often said, must wait upon the repentance of the evil-doer, and until he has showed evidence of that repentance there is no room for love in our treatment of him.

Behind all this readiness to limit the scope of the Christian demand for love lies the powerful but unmentioned influence of Confucian teaching. The scope of the human duty to love is not a new question in Chinese thinking, brought on by the conflict between Christian and Communist doctrine. It is a question that was warmly discussed more than two thousand years ago, when Mo-tzu's call to universal love was sharply condemned by the Confucian school, who maintained that there must be gradations in our affections and attitudes, ranging from filial love toward our parents to justice for our enemies. This traditional Con-

fucian conception still has its appeal, and in the 1930's, before the present Communist question had arisen, a Chinese
Christian professor of philosophy in the Christian University of Nanking presented a paper stoutly maintaining that
the Confucian conception of a graduated system of duties
toward others was superior to the undiscriminating Christian
call for love to all. With this teaching in the background
of their thinking, it is natural that Christians in China today should accept it as not only their patriotic but also
their Christian duty to "discriminate between friend and
enemy"—a phrase used literally hundreds of times in
Christian magazine articles, where the missionaries along
with all of Western imperialism are classified as the enemy.

An instructive example of adaptation of traditional Christian doctrine to current Communist teaching can be found
in an article by Professor Hsieh Shou-ling in *Tien Feng*
magazine for August 6, 1956. Professor Hsieh is a Lutheran,
trained in the West, a competent scholar, and the translator
into Chinese of such standard works as Williston Walker's
Church History. In this article he gives an unusual interpretation of the word "faith," in answer to Peking evangelist Wang Ming-tao, who constantly quoted the verse, "What
has a believer in common with an unbeliever?" as justification for non-co-operation with Communists and with modernist Christians. Mr. Hsieh points out that the meaning of
belief and unbelief here must be determined by the other
contrasts referred to in the passage (2 Cor. 6:14, 15), namely righteousness and iniquity, light and darkness, Christ
and Belial. Of course a Christian should not go along with

one whose life is characterized by unbelief, iniquity, darkness, and Belial. But this sort of belief is more a matter of deeds than of words—just as Jesus approves, not those who say Lord, Lord, but those who do the will of God, and even persons who, like the Good Samaritan, were outside the Jewish faith. Thus Hsieh comes close to discarding the traditional Lutheran doctrine of justification by faith alone, proclaiming instead a justification by works.

The otherworldly note in Christian teaching is another aspect that Chinese Christians are now sharply challenging. Traditionally the otherworldly note has been associated with a recognition of this world as evil, beyond reformation, and steadily growing more evil. But now Chinese society is rapidly moving toward the complete implementation of Communist theoretical principles—that is, toward an ideal state—and therefore the world, or at least the Communist world, must not be thought of as evil and growing more evil. There is a "pollyanna" air of unreality about many of the comments that Chinese Christians make at this point, occasioned by the need to express a rosy optimism in situations that must obviously be full of dark forebodings.

In line with the this-worldly note in present day Christian teaching in China is a strong activist emphasis. Any teaching that glorifies the virtue of patient resignation is now taboo. For example, Mrs. Charles E. Cowman's book of devotional readings *Streams in the Desert*, which in its Chinese translation has had a wide reading, has now been definitely condemned as reactionary in its tendencies. The

Cowmans were former missionaries to Japan and Korea who had to return home when Mr. Cowman was afflicted with an incurable disease. It was during the period when he was slowly dying that Mrs. Cowman compiled the materials in this book. Naturally the call to Christians to accept pain, suffering, and sorrow as the will of God and a means of spiritual discipline is a note that bulks rather large. Some Chinese Christians affirmed that they had found the book very helpful, noting that even in the most ideal societies there would still be such things as incurable diseases that one must be ready to accept in a Christian spirit of submission to the will of God. But it was finally decided that in a "progressive" society there are no evils so inevitable that man's only duty toward them is one of submission; therefore, a book stressing this note was a bad influence.

One of the stock Communist heresies is "reformism," the idea that the evils of society can be cured by a program of gradual reformation. All Christian social teaching that is outside the Communist orbit can be classed as reformism; the more nearly it seems to approach Communist teaching in its specific recommendations, the more vehemently it is denounced by Communists, because it offers an alternative to the Communist demand for revolution. Helen Djang's condemnation of mission schools and Y. T. Wu's of Sherwood Eddy's interpretation of Christian ethics in terms of social action find their justification at this point, namely, that they offer a Christian alternative to revolution, thus blunting the edge of revolutionary fervor.

In all these revisions of Christian teaching, there is the

obvious purpose of harmonizing them as far as possible with Communist doctrine. It is to be noted, however, that at the crucial point of belief in God there is no attempt to blur the antithesis between theism and atheism. The most that is said is that the imperialists try to use that antithesis to create ill feeling between Communists and Christians; whereas, in fact, the antithesis does not constitute a barrier to joint effort for the construction of the New China.

One attempt at such a harmonization, which is yet exceedingly frank in the recognition of the disagreements that exist, is an article by Edmund Hsu in *Tien Feng* magazine, February, 1950. Hsu begins by pointing out three crucial differences between Communist and Christian doctrine, their teaching regarding creation, history, and the control of life. As to creation, the Communists say that everything comes from matter by a dialectical process, whereas Christianity teaches that everything comes from God's creative power. The Communist view of history is that there is a deterministic movement in history from original communism through the stages of slavery, feudalism, and capitalism until the final perfected stage of communism is reached. Christianity teaches instead that all history is under the control of God and finds its meaning only in Christ. The Communists say that the most important, though not the only factor in the control of life, is economics. Christianity makes faith the dominating factor.

Both Christianity and communism look toward a better world; consequently, Mr. Hsu suggests, there must be some points of contact between them. Since history shows us that Christian faith has at various times joined itself with Platonism, Aristotelianism, and rationalism, one may well inquire if there is not a possibility of a similar harmonization with communism.

Here Mr. Hsu finds one positive point of agreement, namely, in the idea of service. The Communists preach and practice service to the people, and there is at least one sentence in Jesus' teaching to which they can raise no objection: "I came not to be ministered unto but to minister." On the basis of this principle Chinese Christians can come to terms with communism. "We have been accustomed to a capitalistic society, but now we have an opportunity to learn more deeply the meaning of that word of Jesus, 'Not those who say Lord, Lord, but those who do the will of the Father shall enter into the Kingdom of Heaven.'"

This crediting of the Communists with unselfish motives of service to the common people is universally present in all discussions of the subject by Chinese Christians. In Y. T. Wu's interpretation, the priest and Levite typify the religious people of the world who pass by on the other side, the Samaritan typifies the nonreligious people, that is, the Communists, who stop to minister to human need. Some Western commentators have identified communism with the Assyria of the Old Testament—"Ho, Assyria, the rod of mine anger," thus making it a terrible scourge that God sends in punishment. Chinese Christians reject that identification, and choose instead to identify communism with the benevolent King Cyrus, of whom the prophet says, "I have called thee, though thou hast not known me."

Indoctrination Through Participation

As Y. T. Wu points out in his article, there is an organic relation between faith and works, between theory and practice, and the Communist government, besides seeking a theoretical *rapprochement* with the Christian church, has taken great pains to establish a mutual working relationship. This shows itself first in official recognition and representation. In the Chinese Communist system representation in the people's congresses at the various levels is not on a purely geographical basis as in the American system, but includes representation of distinct social groups. Christians are sitting as regular members of these people's congresses at every level, from the national congress on down. They usually find occasion in every session of the congress to make at least one speech in which they report on the general situation in the church, and thus there is more official recognition in this regime than in any preceding one that the church has a legitimate position in society.

This recognition has been very useful in alleviating the conditions under which the church works. In 1949 there were many local areas where overzealous Communist officials disregarded the guarantees of religious liberty in their treatment of local churches. That fall Y. T. Wu and two or three others, who were all members of the Chinese People's Political Consultative Congress that had just met in Peking, made a tour through several Central China provinces inspecting church conditions. Wherever these unfair conditions existed they were able to present a protest to the local authorities, and their prestige as members of the honored CPPCC guaranteed that their protests would be given a respectful hearing. This official recognition continues today, and serves to protect the church from extremes of unfair discrimination, though, of course, the church is never exempted from the demands that are made upon society as a whole.

Christian leaders also were called upon to assist in the Land Redistribution Program, along with their fellow citizens. In 1951 the Changchow officials in Fukien province asked for volunteers to help in land redistribution. The local church council recruited forty-three Christians for this purpose; ten of them were preachers or theological students, and the rest were educated laymen. On November 20, when they returned home after two and a half months' work in the villages, they were honored in a special meeting of welcome in one of the Changchow churches. The local Three Self chairman congratulated them on having helped one hundred thousand people turn over a new leaf, saying that thus they had served not only the government and the people, but also the church and their God.

Kiang Wen-han, a Y.M.C.A. national secretary in Shanghai, has given us the most detailed account of what a Christian was called upon to do. Shanghai contributed about two hundred intelligentsia to assist in the land redistribution, and Kiang Wen-han was one of eleven Christians in this group. After three days of briefing sessions in Shanghai, they went out to the villages where they were to work. Kiang with two others, neither of them Christian, was assigned to a village committee consisting of these three intelligentsia from Shanghai, three Communist party members, and thirteen local peasants, some of the latter being illiterate men and women. These nineteen lived and worked together. In the mornings they studied, planned, made reports, and discussed things with each other; in the afternoons they visited homes and fields; in the evenings they held various kinds of public meetings. Each member of the committee was advisor to one section of the countryside—Kiang's section included thirty-five families.

After about two months of preparatory educational work, the group proceeded to classify all the people in their area, confiscate the land of the landlords, make out the redistribution plan, and confirm this plan with the necessary formal acts. In the confiscation step the landlords were required to bring their deeds and turn them over to the people. Some who had been very ruthless with their tenants were dealt with severely, but Kiang does not indicate that any of them were put to death. Finally he lists the three most important impressions that the experience left with him: (1) the sad condition of the peasants before land reform; (2) the fairness and devotedness of the Communists in carrying through this reform; and (3) in contrast, the ineffectiveness of the reformism that Christians had taught before.

Thus by a twofold process of diligent study of Communist theory and active participation in Communist government and economic reorganization, the majority of Christian leaders in China were won over to a firm and in some cases an enthusiastic support of their new political leaders.

A Modus Vivendi

We have just seen something of the process by which leading Chinese Christians were won over to a support of the People's Republic. The roster of those leaders—men recognized as Christian leaders back in Nationalist days, before the coming of the Communists—includes the top men in almost every Protestant denomination. They vary, of course, in the degree of their enthusiasm for the new regime, and some undoubtedly accepted it very reluctantly.

Supporters of the Communist Government

The Y.M.C.A. and the Y.W.C.A. were organizations in which the social gospel had had great vogue, and it is not too surprising to find most of their national secretaries heartily welcoming the new regime. As we have already seen, one of their number, Y. T. Wu, became the leading figure in the new church, and his colleagues Y. C. Tu, Kiang Wen-han, and Liu Liang-mo loyally backed him up. The

Y.W.C.A. National Secretary Cora Deng also has been identified with all the activities of the Three Self Reform Movement from its inception.

In the Methodist Church (American) the senior bishop was Z. T. Kaung. He signed the Manifesto of 1950 and worked actively in the Three Self Movement until his death in 1958. The Sheng Kung Hui (Anglican Church) similarly fell into line. Its presiding bishop was Robin Chen, a man who originally had qualms about the Three Self Movement and refused to sign the Manifesto in 1950. Later, however, he joined the organization and became very prominent in it. Another supporter, even more widely known throughout the world, is Dr. T. C. Chao, who became one of the six presidents of the World Council of Churches when it was organized in 1948. Dr. Chao was originally a Methodist, and had made a name for himself as a Christian scholar while on the faculty of Soochow University. Later he became dean of the interdenominational Yenching School of Religion, joined the Sheng Kung Hui, and was ordained. In 1949 and 1950 he was very active in speaking throughout the country, encouraging the church to accept the social program of the People's Republic. His prestige did much to pave the way for the work of the Three Self Reform Movement.

The outstanding leader in the Church of Christ in China was the Rev. H. H. Ts'ui, its general secretary. He like Dr. Chao was originally a Methodist, but unlike Dr. Chao he remained a Methodist, even though acting as the general secretary of a sister denomination. Incidentally, this anomalous action of a great denomination inviting as its general secretary a pastor from a different denomination will show the Western reader how little the separate denominational traditions of the West amount to in the atmosphere of one of the younger churches. Dr. Ts'ui was active in the work of the Three Self Movement from the outset.

The Rev. Marcus Cheng is another church leader widely known in the West. Of Swedish Lutheran background, Mr. Cheng in his younger days was an active roving evangelist and a fervent preacher of a conservative Christian faith. He worked independently of any of the older established denominations and founded his own theological seminary in Chungking, West China. This school worked in harmonious co-operation with the China Inland Mission. Mr. Cheng was one of the most vigorous proponents of the Three Self Movement in its early days, upholding its point of view and its denunciations with a vigor that shocked many of his milder mannered friends. His participation weakened the argument of those both in China and abroad who maintained that the Three Self Movement was the expression of a modernist, watered down type of Christianity, for he has always stood firmly in the conservative, or even fundamentalist camp.

These are the best known abroad among the supporters of the Three Self Movement, but others of similar standing in the church in China might be named. T. C. Bau was the leading Baptist preacher in Chekiang Province, K. K. Hsiao, the leading Methodist (British) preacher in Hupeh, and Luther Shao, the general secretary of the Christian (Disciples) Church in Nanking. All of these enrolled in the Three Self Movement, and worked actively for its success.

Younger leaders, who only came to prominence since 1949, should also be named here. Of these the most important is K. H. Ting, a Sheng Kung Hui bishop. Dr. Ting was born in Shanghai in 1915, and after college and seminary work at St. John's University in Shanghai, he became student work secretary of the Shanghai Y.M.C.A. After serving in this capacity from 1938 to 1946 he came to America, where he studied in Union Theological Seminary in New York and served a period as secretary of the Canadian student movement. His advancement after his return to China was rapid. After a short period of Y.M.C.A. work, he became secretary of the Christian Literature Society, and then was called to the presidency of Nanking Union Theological Seminary. Shortly afterwards he was elected a bishop of his church and assigned to the Chekiang diocese, which he has administered concurrently with his seminary responsibility. He is a man of deep spiritual perception, and, as we shall see later, is not afraid to speak out boldly on behalf of his Christian faith. In spite of that, he has been a firm upholder of the whole Three Self Movement and has become one of its most trusted spokesmen.

Another new leader is the Rev. Chao Fu-san, also an Anglican priest and a theological professor in Peking. This young man had been a Methodist Y.M.C.A. secretary. He joined the Sheng Kung Hui and was ordained about 1950, after the Communist government had taken over. He immediately attracted attention by the freshness and vigor

22864

with which he defended both the Christian faith and the social program of the government. Like most of those named above, he speaks English fluently, and all the Western visitors to Peking who are interested in the fate of the Chinese churches have interviewed him and been deeply impressed by his sincerity and earnestness. No one who has heard him speak or read his writings has doubted the reality of his Christian convictions. His advocacy has been very influential in establishing the right of the Three Self Movement to speak for the Chinese Christian church.

The Rev. Huang P'ei-yung is a Methodist pastor in Shanghai, who like Chao Fu-san entered the ministry by way of a Y.M.C.A. secretaryship. He is a product of the Foochow Methodist Church, and his brother Huang P'ei-hsin is equally influential, having taken over the direction of Marcus Cheng's seminary in Chungking when the latter retired because of age. Huang P'ei-yung was ordained in Shanghai in 1956, and has become another of the leading spokesmen for the Three Self Movement.

This is an impressive list of church leaders who are active and even enthusiastic backers of the Three Self effort toward a *rapprochement* between the Chinese Christian church and the People's Republic. Such a list makes it impossible to condemn out of hand the Three Self Movement as a betrayal of the Christian faith. One may believe that they are mistaken, that their involvement in the immediate situation has blinded them to the ultimate danger of the road they have taken, but one cannot deny the sincerity of their conviction that in promoting the Three Self

Movement they are continuing to bear witness to the truth of the Christian gospel.

It is true, of course, that most of our news of the China church comes from members of the Three Self Movement. They are the recognized representatives of the Christian church. No one else dares speak, or if he speaks, he cannot get his views published. It is probable, therefore, that the reading of the official Three Self magazine, *Tien Feng*, produces a more massive impression of support for the Three Self Movement than actually exists.

Non-Supporters and Their Fate

Have there been equally sincere and devoted Christians on the other side, critical of and opposed to the Three Self Movement? Yes, there have been a number of these. Let us look at some of them.

W. Y. Ch'en, bishop of the Methodist Church (American), was one of the first victims of the purge that began in 1951. He was imprisoned in March, 1951, and kept in prison for five years. Since his release, either because of continuing house arrest or broken health, he has not been able to resume his work. He was never active in opposition to the Three Self Movement, and even signed the 1950 Manifesto, but he was known as lukewarm toward this nationalistic expression of Christianity. His imprisonment, it is claimed, was not due to his opposition to this movement, but rather to the closeness of his relations with Chiang Kai-shek during and after the Second World War. But a question mark must certainly be raised, not only against a government that imprisons one of its most able and respected citizens but also against the members of a movement who join in the hue and cry over one whom shortly before they had been proud to call a colleague.

Bishop Ch'en's political connections may perhaps explain, even though they do not wholly condone, the action taken against him. But what shall we say of the persecution of the evangelist Wang Ming-tao? Wang Ming-tao was a Peking preacher who was often absent from his church because he was in such great demand all over the country as an evangelist. I remember his coming to Nanking for a series of meetings in a Methodist church there, crowding the church night after night with congregations that hung spellbound on his every word as he preached sermons from an hour and a half to two hours long. He was belligerently fundamentalist in his theology, and since the leader of the Three Self Movement, Y. T. Wu, was a decided liberal, he would have nothing to do with it. As the pressure increased to join the movement as a patriotic expression, he reiterated his stand against any union with modernist thinking, quoting such Scriptures as "What partnership have righteousness and iniquity?"

The Three Self Movement held a nation-wide conference in Peking in July, 1954, at which time several church leaders labored with Mr. Wang, trying to persuade him to join the movement. But he was adamant, they could not move him. The next step was to hold an accusation meeting denouncing him. This took place in September. All church organizations in Peking received orders to have representatives present at this meeting. Mr. Wang was placed on the platform, where he sat with his eyes on the ceiling, never saying a word. Speech after speech was made denouncing him, calling him a traitor, and demanding that the government punish him severely.

This attempt, however, was abortive. Popular feeling was on Mr. Wang's side and the charges against him were too vague for the government to act on. After the harrowing experience of this denunciation meeting, therefore, he was freed and allowed to continue his work. Now his congregations were larger than ever. In the cold of winter they overflowed into the courtyard outside the church, where people stood listening to the service over a loudspeaker. His magazine the *Spiritual Food Quarterly* continued its blasts against the Three Self Movement, accusing its leaders of forsaking Christian truth and preaching atheism. In 1954 he preached a sermon against the movement, entitling it "Betraying the Son of Man with a Kiss," and on August 7, 1955, returned to this theme in a sermon on the text, "They in this manner betrayed Jesus."

But that was his last public utterance. Ever since the unsuccessful attack on Mr. Wang the previous year, the Three Self Movement had been carrying on a campaign to change the trend of popular feeling. The charges against him were clarified and intensified, with the result that on August 8, 1955, the government considered that it could now move against him. He was arrested, and spent a year in prison, during which time two persuasive exponents of communism were in the same cell with him all the time, constantly arguing with him. The next year he was released from prison, but so completely broken in health that he was never able to resume work. At the time of his release a statement was published in the papers that purported to be his confession. It began: "I am a counterrevolutionary offender. As a result of the patient attitude shown by the government and the re-education given me I have come to realize my errors. I have been accorded generous treatment by the government and have been saved from the abyss of crime. For this my heart is full of gratitude." Later, when he was able to make himself heard, he repudiated this statement, and it is not clear whether he had ever in a moment of weakness authorized it or whether it was just a statement put in his mouth by his persecutors. He was returned to prison for a period and then the government released him under house arrest.

This is one of the most clear-cut cases of religious persecution that has come out of China. A recent spokesman for the Three Self Movement has made the claim that Mr. Wang was imprisoned, not because he opposed the movement, but because he was engaged in espionage, a political offense. But this is nonsense. Not even the purported confession referred to above contains any reference to or confession of espionage, which it certainly must have done if that had been any part of the charges against him. No, his crime was purely and simply that he opposed the Three Self Movement, and since this was recognized as a patriotic movement, any opponent of it must be a traitor.

In view of these experiences, a prayer of Martin Luther's

that Mr. Wang quoted in an issue of the *Spiritual Food Quarterly* has added poignancy:

Almighty and Eternal God, how fearful is this world, as it bares its great teeth to eat one up. How weak my heart is as it rests in Thee. My God, help me that I may resist the wisdom of this world. I plead with Thee to arise and work. This is Thy work and not mine. I have come here not for my own benefit or choice. I have no quarrel with these rulers of the world. I would ask for myself to spend my days in happiness and peace. But the affairs of this day are for Thy cause. Thy cause is just and righteous and everlasting. Lord, help me. Thou art faithful and unchanging. I am trusting no man now. Lord, O Lord, wilt Thou not hear me? Art Thou dead? Indeed not, but Thou hast hid Thyself. Lord, my God, where art Thou? Come. Come. Thou hast already chosen me to do the work of this day, and this I know. Now I am ready. Ready to give my life for Thy truth. I am weak as a lamb. The world is filled with devils; though for punishment they put me in the stocks and tear me to pieces and cut me up, though they burn me to ashes, yet is my life with Thee. To this I have already received Thy word as pledge that is sure. Amen. Lord, I pray Thee help me. Amen.

It is also possible that a hymn that came out of Peking in 1953, attracting considerable attention in the United States, was written by Wang Ming-tao. This hymn begins by challenging the Communist claim that "labor creates everything" with a reminder of the Christian doctrine of creation, and then in the second stanza reminds us that God is ever the same, regardless of the changes in the world around us. The translation of this hymn as given below has appeared in several collections of hymns.

106

Father, long before creation
   Thou hadst chosen us in love;
And that love, so deep, so moving,
   Draws us close to Christ above.
     Still it keeps us,
     Still it keeps us,
   Firmly fixed in Christ alone.

Though the world may change its fashion,
   Yet our God is e'er the same;
His compassion and His covenant
   Through all ages will remain.
     God's own children,
     God's own children,
   Must forever praise His name.

God's compassion is my story,
   Is my boasting all the day;
Mercy free and never failing
   Moves my will, directs my way.
     God so loved us,
     God so loved us,
   That his only Son He gave.

Loving Father, now before Thee
   We will ever praise Thy love;
And our song will sound unceasing
   Till we reach our home above,
     Giving glory,
     Giving glory,
   To our God and to the Lamb.[1]

In the heated and intolerant atmosphere that has pre-

[1] Translated in 1953 by F. P. Jones. This hymn can be sung in English to any 8787447 tune, such as Cwm Rhondda.

vailed in China, it occasionally happened that persons were imprisoned against whom there really was no ground for charges. Two of these were the Sheng Kung Hui bishop Kimber Den and the Church of Christ in China scholar Dr. Baen Lee, who at one time was president of Hangchow University, and at the time of his arrest was secretary of the China Bible House. Both of these men were later released by the government with an admission that their imprisonment had been a mistake, but it is noteworthy that the Three Self Movement organ *Tien Feng* was so subservient to the government that at the time of their arrest it claimed that the charge of their being imperialist agents had been fully proved.

Some of the most severe actions of the government have been against indigenous church leaders, men with no connection with any mission board abroad. One of the first of these to suffer was Ching Tien-ying, the founder of the Jesus Family. Late in 1952 he was arrested, and leaders of the Three Self Movement were sent in to reorganize the Jesus Family into conventional type churches, with all the features of communal living obliterated. Mr. Ching was charged with being dictatorial, which he probably was—who could develop a whole new religious movement as rapidly as he had done without being a very decisive character?—and also with being an adulterer, which he probably was not. The real ground of the action against him was the Communist principle that there can be only one pattern of communal living and only one dictator in a Communist state. All others must be liquidated. This action was an embarrassment to some Three Self Movement leaders who had earlier praised the Jesus Family program very highly, as a Christian expression of Communist principles. Now they had to publish articles in which they retracted their former statements and pointed out how they had been deceived.

Another indigenous church leader to be imprisoned was Watchman Nyi, the founder of the Little Flock. He and two of his associates were arrested in April, 1952, and he has been in prison ever since. Then in January, 1956, further action was taken against this church, first in Shanghai and then in other cities, at which time so many of the Little Flock leaders were imprisoned that it became necessary to have a complete reorganization of the church. The charges against them were of "carrying on destructive activities, breaking down government policies and central movements, scattering reactionary words and counter revolutionary rumors, instilling fear into the hearts of church members, poisoning the minds of youth, and destroying the unity of the Christian church in opposing imperialism and in love for country and church." (Quotation from *Tien Feng* editorial.) That is to say, they exhorted their members not to co-operate with the government or with the Three Self Movement.

The leaders of the True Jesus Church were also attacked. The founder Paul Wei was no longer living, but his son Isaac Wei was now one of the leaders of this church, and he was early put in prison. Later several leaders from this church's headquarters in the Wuhan cities were imprisoned. The published charges against them are concerned mostly with their attempts at faith healing, which it was charged resulted in the death of many victims, and with the ecstatic nature of their worship, which was said to be unscientific and harmful. But there could hardly have been such a general liquidation of this church's leaders if it had not been believed that they were definitely anti-government in their attitude.

In every one of these cases of harassment of prominent church leaders, the spokesmen of the Three Self Movement rallied to the defense of the government, pointing out that the action against these churchmen was due to political reasons and had nothing to do with their faith, and that therefore the official government policy of "freedom of religious belief" had not been flouted. In a sense this is true. These men suffered, not because they were Christian leaders, but because they stood in the way of the government program, just as a banker or a merchant who stood in the way of that program also suffered. But to say that therefore it is no infringement of the freedom of religious belief is to betray a very narrow view of religion, a view that limits it to speculative propositions and ritual acts.

Here, then, we have two wings of the Christian movement in China, the patriotic and nationalistic wing led by Y. T. Wu and the Three Self Movement, and the individualistic wing typified by Wang Ming-tao. The former is in effective control and the latter persecuted and imprisoned. It is a situation reminiscent of many periods in church history when free churches have battled against the pretensions of state churches. Wang Ming-tao may be seen as another George Fox, battling for freedom of conscience in the face of the totalitarian demands of the state church, and Y. T. Wu as an Oliver Cromwell who looks upon the imprisonment of such an individualist as a pious act. And just as in those parlous days of the seventeenth century, when each side denied the Christian profession of the other, so it is today. Both inside and outside China the partisans of each group insist that only its side is truly Christian and the other side is apostate.

Western Attitudes

This denunciation of the Three Self leaders and all the churches connected with them as apostate is to be found in the West especially among those with a conservative theological outlook. We have seen that the former China Inland Mission missionary Leslie Lyall calls the 1950 Manifesto a manifesto of betrayal. The conservative magazine *Christianity Today* uniformly takes the same attitude, while the ultraconservative Reformed Presbyterian missionary Samuel Boyle, who formerly worked in China but is now stationed in Japan, goes so far as to deny the very name of church to all the churches associated together in the Three Self Movement, that is, all the Protestant churches in China today.

Another group that joins in this denunciation is composed of those with a political motivation. It is natural that all who believe strongly that the Nationalist government in Taiwan is the rightful government of China should also feel that mainland citizens who submit to the iniquitous and atheistic Communist government are traitors to their own best selves, and certainly unworthy to bear the name of Christian.

The Western Christians who uphold the Three Self Movement can also in general be grouped into two main groups. There is first the group of those who believe strongly in the social gospel, even to the extent of condoning the excesses committed in the name of a forward social program. The best known of this group is the "Red Dean" of Canterbury Cathedral, Hewlett Johnson, who has visited China since Liberation several times and always has the highest words of praise for the Three Self Movement. Another example is a former missionary of the United Church of Canada, James Endicott, who was one of the recipients of the Stalin Peace Prize. He is a leader in the Communist oriented world peace movement and naturally supports the Three Self Movement and condemns its critics.

The second group of Western supporters of the Three Self Movement is composed of those whose thinking is accustomed to accommodate itself to the inclusive thinking of a state church. It has been aptly said that when the meek inherit the earth they inherit a lot of problems that a meek man can't handle, so when a church becomes a state church it inevitably compromises the purity of Christian ideals. This, Ernst Troeltsch has pointed out in his great work *The Social Teaching of the Christian Churches,* is the price that a church has to pay in order to achieve the comprehensiveness characteristic of a state church. In contrast to the state church, the sect or free church can be as unrealistic as it pleases in the espousing of ideals that have no chance of acceptance by the body politic. This type of inclusive church thinking is more characteristic of England and the Continent than of American Christianity, and so we find that the British Anglican, David Paton, and the German missions scholar, Walter Freytag, have neither of them any scruples about accepting the leaders of the Three Self Movement as valid representatives of the Christian church.

Freytag has in addition a peculiarly poignant basis for sympathy with the leaders of the Three Self Movement from the analogy with the German church leaders of the Hitler period. These latter were constantly meeting the attitude in other Christian nations that any true German Christian ought to be in prison; if he was still at large, that was prima-facie evidence that he was not a true Christian. And so, remembering how grieved German Christians were at meeting this suspicion, he is inclined to sympathize with Y. T. Wu and the other leaders who have been discussed above.

But there is a mediating position possible between these two extremes. We have come to see that it is possible to condemn a specific act as unchristian without thereby denying the essential Christian character of the perpetrator—otherwise who could be called a Christian? And so I believe that we may well regret deeply the spirit of intolerance and hatred that the Christian church in China today has taken over from the Chinese Communist party and yet refrain from impugning the sincerity of their Christian commitment.

Y. T. Wu preached a sermon in Peking in the summer of 1952, a sermon that closed with these words, "Fundamental religion is this—to stand like children before the infinite majesty of God, to adore, depend, and obey." That is a language that speaks to my heart, and I recognize in the speaker a fellow-heir to the promises of Christ.

The Chinese Church and the West

By early 1951 all the missionaries were either out of the country or else completely isolated, cut off from the life of the Chinese church. There were, of course, a few exceptions. Ralph and Nancy Lapwood, because of their sympathetic attitude toward the new regime, were allowed to remain in Peking where they were teaching in a Christian university. These London Missionary Society missionaries finally left in 1952. Harry Gould, a China Inland Mission worker, realizing that it was impossible to remain in China as a missionary, resigned from the Mission and took work in the Shanghai office of a British shipping concern. He was able to keep in some contact with various Christian groups in Shanghai until the shipping concern closed in 1955. Mrs. Margaret Kiesow was an English Presbyterian missionary who was able to stay at Cheeloo University in Shantung Province until September 1953. A retired Danish missionary, Miss Ellen Nielsen, had taken Chinese citizenship and was allowed to remain at her station in Manchuria until her death in 1959. She was, however, quite isolated from the work of the church, and at least part of the time was not even allowed to go to church on Sunday. These few scattered exceptions are enough to show how complete was the severance of relations between the Chinese church and the West.

Here then was the end of an era. After nearly one hundred and fifty years of devoted and sacrificial work the mission boards of the West were completely cut off from the churches that they had succeeded in founding in China. It was the first time that a severance of relations between mother and daughter churches in the modern missionary era had occurred on such a massive scale and with such apparent finality. It was natural that all to whom the cause of Christian missions was dear should be deeply troubled, asking themselves, "What have we done that was wrong, that our work should have been so suddenly cut off? Why couldn't we have prevented this?" Thus the whole missionary program and strategy came under review in an attempt to learn a lesson from the China experience that might help to avoid such a catastrophe in other mission lands.

Lessons from the China Experience

Mission boards in the United States co-operated in a China evaluation study in 1951, a study carried out by a questionnaire and by a three-day consultation. The results were considered too tentative to be published, but a mimeographed report, "Lessons to be Learned from the Experiences of Christian Missions in China," was issued for limited distribution. This cross section of missionary and mission board thinking, while reflecting considerable difference of opinion at many vital points, still gives strong support to the analyses recorded below of Barnabas, Paton, and Hayward. These three analyses have been published, and are worth serious study.

The first of these was the pamphlet by "Barnabas," published in 1951, and entitled *Christian Witness in Communist China*. The author, Charles West, was at that time a young Presbyterian missionary. Since then he has worked with the World Council of Churches in Geneva and is now an associate professor of Christian Ethics at Princeton Theological Seminary. He chose the pseudonym of Barnabas to suggest the proper place of the missionary today as one willing to accept second place, not expecting to be the Paul of the enterprise.

This pamphlet is concerned only incidentally with analyzing and bewailing the past; its more immediate concern is to assure the Western world that Christian witness is still possible in Communist China, and to indicate some of the lines along which it can operate. His program for Christian witness, though ostensibly directed to the readers in the Western world, was undoubtedly also meant for Chinese Christians, thus betraying a hope that missionary influence could still be exerted in the new situation. But it is not likely that more than a mere handful of Chinese Christians have read the pamphlet, and their witness, though real and positive, has not been as independent and free as he suggests it might have been.

For Western Christian readers, the message of Barnabas is a rebuke for having neglected the problems that communism undertakes to solve. The economic oppression of the underprivileged should be a vital concern of the Christian church, he says, but it has not been. In this Christians have not followed the teaching of Jesus. "Marx unquestionably misunderstood the Gospel of Jesus Christ. But we are left with the searching question: Did he misunderstand the churches and the practice of Christians as they exist today?" West insists that no Christian can bear effective witness in a Communist country unless he, too, is concerned with the evils that provide the motivation of Communist activity. Western churches and their missionaries have not been sufficiently concerned with those evils, and as a result the churches that they have built up have found themselves ill prepared to meet the moral challenge of communism. They have been forced in shame and penitence, Barnabas concludes, to learn the principles of economic justice from those whom they have looked down upon as atheists and materialists.

David Paton in his little book *Christian Missions and the Judgment of God* (published in 1953, but composed of lectures delivered in 1952) was more directly concerned with an analysis and criticism of the whole missionary program of the Western churches. Mr. Paton was an Anglican missionary in China and is now secretary of that church's Council of Ecumenical Co-operation. He examines the Communist charge of imperialism and admits a certain truth in it, and also a certain inevitability. It is impossible, Paton says, to preach a "pure gospel," free from all traces of cultural invasion. The very principles of the Incarnation forbid this possibility; the message must be mediated through personalities conditioned by time and place. Perhaps a "theology of imperialism" is needed, though he points out wryly that it may turn out to be a demonology instead. The imperialistic evils inherent in the direction of church life by missionaries from foreign lands might have been avoided, he thinks, if they had taken to heart the program for missionary activity set forth by Roland Allen nearly fifty years ago. Roland Allen in two books *(Missionary Methods: St. Paul's or Ours,* 1912, and *The Spontaneous Expansion of the Church and the Causes Which Hinder It,* 1927) had advocated a policy of leaving young churches on their own as soon as they are organized. Mr. Allen's reasons were biblical (as the subtitle of the first book suggests), logical, and practical. Mr. Paton now adds another reason: It would avoid the danger of imperialist domination of the young church by the missionary, an evil now being loudly denounced in China, but also felt and resented, though not so vocally expressed, in other countries. The missionary is especially useful as a pioneer; after the pioneer period is over, Paton thinks he should get out of the way. The freedom from local ties and social family complications that is an asset to the missionary in the early stages soon becomes a drawback, for it is precisely those ties and complications that need to be redeemed.

Mr. Paton makes a strong plea for the development of a deeper prophetic insight into the meaning of historic cataclysms. The Communists in China have been considered under three very different biblical figures: the Assyrians of Isaiah 10, the rod of God's anger unwittingly fulfilling the will of God in judgment; the Cyrus of Isaiah 45, beneficently bringing liberation to God's people; the beast of the Apocalypse and the harlot drunk with the blood of the saints. These varying interpretations, all by Christians as they look at China, suggest to Paton that one of the prime needs for missionary statesmanship today is an ability to read the signs of the times, with its corollary of an adequate understanding of the relations of church and state, especially at the point where these relations affect missionary work.

Victor E. W. Hayward, formerly an English Baptist missionary in China, and now the general secretary of the Baptist Missionary Society, put out (in 1955) a booklet *Ears to Hear: Lessons from the China Mission* that sums up the lessons to be learned from the China experience in a very perceptive and systematic way. First, there must come a recognition that there were certain failures in missionary strategy. Mission boards and missionaries laid themselves open to the charge of political imperialism when they became the beneficiaries of the "Unequal Treaties," the nineteenth century treaties between China and the West. These treaties are so universally condemned by the Chinese that to be a beneficiary of them is to be *ipso facto* an aggressor against China. Mr. Hayward draws the very valid conclusion that we must "scrutinize with the utmost care all Mission-Government relations, balancing immediate advantage against long-term consequences." Mission policies also encouraged a sort of cultural imperialism. Missionaries who lacked an appreciation of Chinese culture often directed the policies of mission schools to such an extent that the schools "denationalized" their pupils.

Missionaries, Mr. Hayward says, were inclined to remain in control of church life and organization too long, and here he repeats Mr. Paton's call for a restudy of Roland Allen's contribution to sound mission policy. Again, he criticizes the approach referred to by Y. T. Wu, that is, to "preach Christ as the way to a powerful and self-respecting new China." We must, he says, never preach Christianity as a means to an end, but rather preach it as "the eternal truth offering men life and demanding their obedience simply because it is true."

Mr. Hayward also believes that too much of the missionary's limited resources went into schools and hospitals and other forms of social welfare, to the neglect of the inner life of the church itself. When the Communists came to power all these institutions were taken away from the church. Then the church was reduced to that which is its primary reason for existence, namely, the preaching of the gospel and the nurturing of the spiritual life of its members. Moreover, so many of these institutions were established that they had had to be partially manned with non-Christian personnel, and this seriously affected their witness to the gospel.

Finally, he charges missionaries with having failed in spiritual identification with the people among whom they

121

worked. Too many of the missionaries remained lifelong aliens in a culture that they took little pains to understand or appreciate. "The prophet Ezekiel declared, 'I sat where they sat': the emissary of Christ must do no less."

All of these criticisms are valid, and moreover, they are equally relevant to missionary work in other countries. Take, for example, the charge that missionaries are inclined to maintain control of the younger churches too long. Some years ago an African Christian showed that the same situation exists there, and is equally resented by African Christians, by the use of a little parable that though delightfully good-humored yet packs its own sting. He said, "Once an African went out into the forest and shot an elephant. In great glee he returned to his village and said, 'I have shot an elephant. Come and help me drag it home, and we'll all have lots of meat to eat.' So they went out to where the elephant was lying and attached ropes to his legs and started to pull. For this they had to co-ordinate their efforts, and to help in this co-ordination they improvised, as Africans will, a little song. The words were very simple, just intoning 'Our elephant, our elephant.' But then the group noticed that the man who shot the elephant was singing different words. 'What is this you are singing?' they asked. 'My elephant, my elephant,' came the reply. 'I shot him, didn't I?' 'Well, if it is your elephant, you can pull him in,' they answered, and they dropped the ropes and started to go back home. The man pulled first on one rope and then on another, but he couldn't budge that heavy mass of meat. So finally he ran after the other men and said to them, 'My mistake, it's *our* elephant.' " The missionary often needs to be prodded by a similar incipient revolt before he learns that the church is "our elephant."

Mr. Hayward has a further very perceptive chapter on "Weaknesses We Have Reproduced." The missionary reproduces the church he knew back home, with all its weaknesses, and these include a comparative ignorance of theology, an ignorance of the true meaning of the church, a failure to make the church a true fellowship, and a neglect of stewardship teaching. Most serious of all, the missionary in China reproduced the Western church's "relative lack of concern for social righteousness." Individual missionaries have in their work transcended these points of weakness, but the mission program as a whole cannot do so until the sending church, the church in the West, has learned to correct them.

Finally, Mr. Hayward boldly exhorts the church to learn from the Communists, whom he considers to be the outstanding missionaries of today. By and large, they have been "out-thinking, out-living and out-dying Christians." The points in their strategy that he finds to be worth emulating are: They know the strength that comes from unity. They make a maximum demand upon their members. They have skill in propaganda, both public and in unobtrusive cells. Here he asks, "Why are there not cells of dedicated Christians in schools and factories, shops and government offices, hospitals and trade unions up and down the land using the power of united prayer and witness in fellowship to proclaim the hidden rule of Christ in the world?" Again, Communist advance is planned and carried through in clearly marked stages. Mission work would profit greatly through planning that would tell when to abandon one type of work and move on to another. Finally, Christians, who have the true key to history in the purposes of God, have allowed the Communists to take the initiative in "their professedly scientific interpretation of history and their conviction of sure victory for their cause through alliance with the very processes of history, whereas Christians have often appeared indifferent to what is happening in history, and uncertain and divided as to what end to man's strivings is to be anticipated."

Mr. Hayward, having waited until 1955, was in a better position than either West or Paton to cover the "Lessons from the China Mission" in a truly comprehensive way. He says in the preface that former China missionaries have shown an astonishing measure of agreement as to what these lessons are, which is only true if you are rather easily astonished. However, it is true that almost every one of his points is well taken, and moreover, is relevant to the situation in countries where mission work has not yet been cut off by a Communist revolution.

Repudiation of Colonial Relationships

These analyses just reviewed constitute a sort of post-mortem examination of an era that has come to an end. It is worth emphasizing again, however, that the corpse in this post-mortem is not the church but the mission. The mission has gone, but the church is still alive and active.

That church, in declaring its independence from its former mission board ties, has repudiated all mission board relationships as being a sort of ecclesiastical colonialism. This means that they have not only cut themselves off from the mission boards, but also from the International Missionary Council.

The first great Protestant unification expression in the twentieth century was the Edinburgh Missionary Conference of 1910. From the Conference grew a world-wide organization, the International Missionary Council, in which both sending and receiving churches were represented. The IMC sponsored two great world-wide conferences—the Jerusalem conference of 1928 and the Madras (India) conference of 1938—in which the gradual coming of age of the younger churches is clearly reflected. Later conferences, in Whitby, Ontario, in 1947, in Willingen, Germany, in 1952, and in Ghana, in 1957, were on a smaller scale and less spectacular.

The very construction of the IMC seemed to involve an invidious distinction between the sending and receiving nations. The latter were represented through their Christian Councils, organizations comparable to the National Council of the Churches of Christ in the United States, while the former were represented only through subsidiary agencies of the churches, namely, the mission boards. As might have been expected, the resurgent nationalism of the Chinese church rejected this connection, considering it a part of the imperialistic and colonial psychology of the West.

In contrast to the IMC, the World Council of Churches

admits older and younger churches on a more or less equal basis, though of course the older and larger churches have more influence. This equality encourages Chinese Christians to take a more favorable attitude toward the WCC and to consider themselves as still within that ecumenical fellowship, even though conditions for the time being make it impossible for them to exercise that fellowship. It is true that Dr. T. C. Chao, who was elected in 1948 as one of the six presidents of the WCC, resigned that position in 1952. But his was a personal protest against the action of the Central Committee of the WCC, which approved United Nations intervention in the Korean War (Toronto, Canada, 1950). In spite of Dr. Chao's resignation, some Chinese Christian leaders still considered themselves as belonging to the WCC; they only insisted that they could not exercise their rights of membership as long as the WCC showed itself to be, as they believed, so one-sided in its judgment on international questions.

New Ecumenical Relations

Chinese Christians felt keenly the isolation that the new situation in China had forced upon them, and they tried to overcome it by actions along two lines. First, they established fraternal relations with Christian churches within the Communist family of nations—Russia, Czechoslovakia, and Hungary. Second, and later, they made an effort to re-establish contact with churches in noncommunist lands.

Fraternal relations were established with churches in Communist countries when representatives of these churches were invited to visit China. The Chinese churches in turn sent their representatives to visit these European nations. One report of a delegation of Chinese churchmen to Hungary in November, 1957, is interesting because it shows how completely different their orientation is from ours.

Bishop K. H. Ting tells us what he was thinking of as his airplane approached Budapest: "As we looked down on Budapest from the air, we could not help but think of the dark days a year ago, when the imperialists were carrying on their counterrevolutionary activities. In those days, as we Chinese read the papers, our hearts were very sad, and we asked ourselves, 'Can it be true that Hungary is leaving the Communist family of nations?' But then when the workers' and farmers' revolutionary government was re-established, and Hungary with the help of Soviet Russia was able to suppress so quickly this counterrevolutionary revolt, our hearts were made peaceful again. Looking down from the air, I could not help but think of Luke 15, 'This your brother was dead, and is alive; he was lost, and is found; therefore let us make merry and be glad.'"

Farther on in his report, Bishop Ting comments on Communist government in a way that shows how he could make what seems a blasphemous comparison of the reconquered Hungary with the repentant prodigal son: "Our righteous and merciful God is not indifferent to the oppression and slavery that the people of the world have suffered. Can He then care nothing about the great changes that are taking place under Communist governments? Certainly not. We know that in the parable the priest and Levite may have been zealous in temple worship, but when they saw a man wounded by the roadside they paid no attention to his groans and passed by on the other side. But God is not like them. He is the ruler of heaven and earth, and Christ is the Lord of the whole world. The affairs of communism are certainly not outside the providence of this great God who is Lord of History."

Re-opening Contacts with the West

The Chinese church's attempts at re-establishing relations with the churches in noncommunist countries have been more cautious and tentative, but some hopeful beginnings have been made. In 1954 a secular organization, the All-China Youth Federation, perhaps because of the fact that the Y.M.C.A. and the Y.W.C.A. were members of it, issued an invitation to various church bodies in Great Britain to send visitors to China. There was no church that accepted the invitation as a denomination, but the following bodies decided to accept: Young Friends (Quakers), the Iona Community of the Church of Scotland, the William Temple Association of Anglican Graduates, and Christian Action.

Dr. Marcus James, an Anglican clergyman of Jamaican ancestry, went as a representative of Christian Action, and W. Beverly Burwell as representative of the William Temple Association. They were received very cordially wherever they went, and came back with reports that many missionaries were still remembered with gratitude and affection. And although the criticisms of missionary imperialism were repeated to them (the Canadian Burwell discounted these criticisms but James, with his colonial background, was inclined to acquiesce), Chinese Christian leaders expressed a hope for further fellowship with the churches of the West. Frequently they asked the visitors, "Can it be that Western dislike for the government under which we live is greater than the desire for Christian fellowship with us?"

A delegation of six British Quakers was the next group from abroad to visit the church in China (1955). Here again the invitation itself came not from the church but from the China Peace Committee. This host committee was said to be very considerate in giving the visitors opportunity for discussion and worship with Christian groups. Since two members of the delegation had been missionaries in China they had a better basis for understanding what they saw than complete strangers to the China scene would have had.

The Quakers reported church life as proceeding quite normally, with steady increases in membership beginning to make up for the earlier defection of "rice Christians." The chief activity in most churches, next to worship, was Bible study, and almost every church had weekday evening classes for this purpose. As a result, sale of Bibles by the China Bible House remained brisk, new printings were coming from the press, and there was no limitation on the number that could be printed. The Y.M. and Y.W. organizations were active in carrying on Bible study conferences for young people. On the whole, Christian leaders in China seemed to feel that the loss of foreign aid had been a blessing in disguise: It had increased the sense of responsibility among the Chinese church members who now contributed generously to church expenses, and the fact that the church was now clearly Chinese in management had removed the stigma attached to a "foreign cult."

The Quakers recognized that Chinese Christians were more involved in the life of the nation than formerly, and that this imposed on them, as on all Chinese citizens, certain limitations of thought and action. Wherever persecution of Christian leaders had occurred, they agreed that it was political heresy rather than religious faith that had caused it. Moreover, Chinese Christians like other Chinese were denied access to the political thinking of the West, and their views of world events were inevitably colored by the interpretations in the Communist press. The Quaker delegation stressed that this difference in viewpoint must be kept in mind when the time comes for the resumption of fellowship between Chinese Christians and the West. The delegation believed, however, that the deep desire of Chinese Christians for that resumption gave assurance that the differences that seem to separate us can be overcome.

This report was embodied in a booklet *Quakers Visit China,* and a copy of it was sent to Congregational minister P. H. Wang in Peking. He was deeply disappointed in the book, and wrote a letter to its editor, Gerald Bailey, to tell him so. Although it had seemed to outside observers to be a warm and friendly statement, Mr. Wang found in it the "atmosphere of cold war." This is an indication of a peculiar psychology existing among Chinese Christians today. They are very free in making violent denunciations of missionaries and of the West, but cannot stand any criticism of themselves whatever, and anyone making such criticism is said to be raising an insuperable barrier to East-West fellowship.

The first official church visit from the free world to the church in China came in November, 1956, when Anglican Archbishop Howard W. K. Mowll of Australia, in response to an invitation from Bishop Robin Chen, presiding bishop of the Chung Hua Sheng Kung Hui, led a delegation of eight Australian Anglicans on an extended visit throughout China. The Sunday after their arrival in Shanghai Archbishop Mowll preached in the Anglican cathedral to a congregation of over six hundred, and the visitors concluded that it must have been a congregation of regular churchgoers, for they sang hymns and service with zest.

In Peking one member of the delegation, Francis James, had an interview with Ho Chen-hsiang, the 54-year-old director of the Religious Affairs Bureau. Mr. Ho insisted that the government welcomed criticism, and that the church was encouraged to criticize the government "in a constructive way." Mr. James replied, "If all is as you say, then why are there so many Christian leaders still in prison? To my certain knowledge there are four Roman Catholic bishops and three Protestants. And Wang Ming-tao and our own Bishop Kimber Den have only just been released from jail. If that is not religious persecution, then what is it?"

In answer Mr. Ho maintained that each of these men was supposed to have committed some political offense, consequently their imprisonment was not due to religious persecution. He admitted that Bishop Kimber Den's imprisonment had been an injustice. "I can only say that we welcome your criticisms over this, and that those who were responsible for the delays, which are the most unsatisfactory aspect of the case, have been severely punished." He went on, however, to excuse the "many unfortunate things" of that sort that had happened by saying that they were a "natural reaction by many Chinese people after the things that had been done against China under the guise of missionary work."

When asked about freedom to preach the gospel, Mr. Ho stated that the only thing prohibited was open air meetings, and there were special reasons for this. But, he added, "they have all sorts of legitimate avenues apart from that. They have their services. They have meetings in halls and churches, literature, personal visits, catechism classes, retreats, meetings in private houses and so on. [Actually, many of these activities have often been severely limited.] They have even this extraordinary custom [here he gave James a knowing wink] of baptizing innocent infants, who do not know what it is all about! Now, a thing like that, although opposed to reason, and however ridiculous it may seem, is after all harmless, and so we have never tried to intervene against it." Mr. James wisely did not try to argue infant baptism with him.

In a meeting with eighteen Christian leaders of Shanghai, the Anglicans found themselves baffled by the wooden and parrot-like nature of the responses to their questions. Mr. James concluded that the only way really to get at the facts would be through private interviews; but somehow, they were never able to arrange for these. This situation has been noted by a number of visitors to China with a special interest in the church. They are able only to interview a selected number of church leaders in each of the large cities, and in these interviews are able to elicit only the same kind of answers everywhere.

An explanation for this was provided by a firsthand report from a Chinese Christian leader who was briefed in preparation for meeting foreign visitors.

He was called one day to the Religious Affairs Bureau of his city, where he found a dozen of his Christian colleagues who had received similar summonses. The Commissioner for Religious Affairs took charge of the meeting and announced that at such and such a time, about a month later, they were to be honored with a visit from a distinguished foreign churchman. "I have been given your names," he went on, "as people who know him personally, and whom, therefore, he will probably want to see when he comes here. I have now called you together that we may consult on how best to answer the questions that he will ask." This first meeting was just a preliminary survey. By the next week, when they were called together again, the Commissioner had more concrete agenda for discussion. He said, "Our visitor has already met with the Christian leaders in Peking, and I have here a list of the questions that he asked them. Here is Question No. 1. Mr. X, if he asked you this question, how would you answer him?" Mr. X thereupon made the answer that he thought the Commissioner expected, and his answer was mulled over, criticized, and amended by the whole group. Finally the Commissioner summed up the discussion by saying, "We are agreed then, that if he asks this question here, we will answer in this way."

And so in a series of meetings all the matters that the visitor was known to be interested in were analyzed and the answers decided upon. Finally the visitor arrived, had a very "informal and frank" discussion for one whole evening with these church leaders, and was duly impressed with the general agreement they showed in regard to the good relations existing between church and government. Of course he had no opportunity to interview any of them separately.

This is a procedure that sounds very strange to Western ears, and it inevitably raises the question, Why is the government unwilling for Christian leaders to make unrehearsed and spontaneous answers to the questions asked of them? Is there some element in the situation that it does not want the outside world to know?

There were also delegations of Japanese and Indian Christians that visited China in 1957. One of the latter asked Anglican Bishop Ting about the church's subservience to the Communists, and was told, "We do not automatically support everything the Communists do. They have done certain things that I regard as extreme and haphazard. Some of these things I later understood to have been quite reasonable, but there are others of whose necessity I remain unconvinced even today."

In addition to these visits of foreign churchmen to China, there have been a few visits by Chinese churchmen abroad, of which the most important are of Bishop Ting to England and Europe in the summer of 1956, of a group of Y.M.C.A. leaders to India in 1957, and of the Rev. Chao Fusan to Australia in 1959. (Mr. Chao's visit to Australia was to a Peace Congress, and not specifically to the church.) Bishop Ting's visit to England was to represent the Sheng Kung Hui in a preparatory meeting for the Lambeth Conference of 1958, and it was expected that several Chinese bishops would come to London for the event. But the situation had so changed by that time that Chinese participation had become impossible. Bishop Ting also attended a meeting of the Central Committee of the World Council of Churches in Hungary as an unofficial observer. (As already pointed out, some Chinese Christian leaders regard their churches as members of the World Council, but they are not ready yet to implement that membership.) As an indication of welcome to this visitor, the Central Committee passed a resolution favoring a visit to China by a World Council delegation "whenever such a visit would be welcome."

The paucity of these official contacts between the churches of China and the West in the years since 1951 is a matter of deep concern and regret to most of those who have worked in China and come to know the Christian church there. A few, however, have protested even these scanty contacts. They would deny the right of the Three Self Reform Movement leaders to speak for the church in China, or to be recognized as church leaders. This is a

135

mistake. Much as we may deplore some of the things that
Y. T. Wu and other church leaders have done, they must
be recognized as devout and earnest Christians. Their caution about reopening contacts with the West they have
themselves explained by likening it to the need for a tariff
to protect infant industries. When the industry is no longer
infant the tariff may be removed, and when the church in
China has carved out its place in Chinese life it may resume fellowship with the churches of the West. In the
meantime the years 1954 to 1957 saw some token manifes-
tations of a renewed fellowship, a fellowship that we may
hope will be broadened when the domestic and foreign
situation permits.

The Hundred Flowers and After

It was noted in Chapter 3 that there was a period of lessening tension in China during 1956 and 1957. This was the time when a "hundred flowers," that is, all schools of thought, were encouraged to bloom. The invitation to freedom of expression was responded to by church leaders with the same promptness as characterized other segments of the population. Sheng Kung Hui Bishop Stephen Chang of Wuhan said publicly, "Now is the time for the faithful to turn the tables." Two years earlier he had complained that the government was making direct attacks on the church, and that "Protestants had to suffer in silence." Several other church leaders in Wuhan (the triple cities in Central China of Hankow, Wuchang, and Hanyang) spoke out charging the Three Self Reform Movement with having co-operated with the government in taking away their political rights. One leader said that the lack of personal freedom under the Communist government was intolerable. Another criticized the church for having taken part in the denunciation campaigns at government behest. This man was a member of the Wuhan Three Self committee, and he tried to get the committee to come out with a public attack on the Communist party.

The veteran evangelist Chia Yü-ming also encouraged criticism in his theological seminary in Shanghai. He himself is reported in his course on the book of Revelation to have declared that those with the mark of the beast on their foreheads typified the members of the Communist party. The false prophet that arose out of Judah (but it is nowhere stated that he arose out of Judah, see Rev. 16:13) was the Jew Karl Marx. In commenting on the second beast that represented the false prophet, Chia made clear that it typified the Communist party, and then said of it that it "made itself great," writing as he did so upon the blackboard the word "itself" above the word "great," which together make up the Chinese character for "It stinks."

One of the members of his faculty challenged Communist atheism with a little poem in which he showed his contempt of their teaching:

> I say, God is; you say No;
> Let's see who will suffer woe.
> You say, No God; I say you're wrong;
> We'll see who sings salvation's song.

Bishop Ting's Witness

After the Hundred Flowers period was over, all the criticisms noted above were duly brought forward as evidence of rightist thinking and used to denounce those who had been so bold. But there is one remarkable production from this period that as far as is known did not arouse any suspicion against the speaker. This was the address Anglican Bishop K. H. Ting, president of Nanking Union Theological Seminary, made to his students on June 12, 1957, just at the end of the free-speaking period. This address was then published in August, in one of the few numbers of the *Seminary Review.* The title of the address was "Christian Theism," and in it he laid down a challenge to materialism in very decided terms. He began by saying, "We know that the various atheistic theories are wrong, but we must also know wherein they are wrong, and still more, what the right view is. We must think deeper and strengthen our faith so that when we go out to preach the truth of the gospel our words may carry weight because of their reasonableness."

The Communists try to divide all systems of thought into the two categories of materialism and idealism, condemning the latter and approving the former. But the bishop replies that to ask such a question of Christianity does not correspond with Christian reality, for Christianity is neither one nor the other. "Other people may ask the question if they like, but we are not obliged to answer." For, as a matter of fact, although Christianity has been deeply influenced by human history, and thus can be thought of under historical categories, yet "in itself it is not the fruit of history, and the gospel is not an ideology. The gospel comes from the free revelation of God. This gospel is Christ himself, through whom all things were made." Thus we

139

must never think of Christianity as just another ideology.

He then proceeds to dispose of the Communist charge that "religion is the opiate of the people." He begins by pointing out that the charge is irrelevant to the question of whether or not God exists. "Let us imagine a man who because of some great grief has become very pessimistic about the world, his country, and his family, and so he seeks an escape from reality, in order to benumb his mind. Is it not possible that such a man might choose astronomy as his opiate? Day and night he might sit at his telescope, drawing calmness of mind from the great emptiness of space. But the fact that he was using astronomy as an opiate would not mean that the sun, the moon, and the stars that he saw through his telescope did not really exist. On the contrary, it is possible that his observations might make a great contribution to the advance of astronomy. His subjective psychological state is one thing, the objective existence of the universe is quite another thing."

But he is not satisfied to leave the question in this ambiguous way. He goes on vigorously to deny that true Christianity is an opiate at all. He points out that Christ even on the cross and in the greatest pain of body refused the opiate drink that a compassionate bystander offered him. "Consider, if he had consented to drink the drug, he might have escaped the pain, but then he would no longer have known what was going on around him, the Seven Great Words from the cross would have been left unsaid, and the meaning of the cross itself would have been dark and unclear." St. Ambrose once inveighed against the rich, saying, "The world was made for all men, how can you claim it as your private property?" Bishop Ting quotes this, and then observes, "The saint who said this was not a man who had been benumbed by some opiate." He also quotes a memorable saying of John Hus, "Woe to me if I keep silent. If I do not speak out against the gravest evils, then I become an accomplice of sin and hell, and it were better had I never been born," and then asks the pertinent question, "Who dares to say that a man who talks like this has been drugged with an opiate?"

How can a man come to know that God exists? The bishop points out that reason and the observation of nature give us a certain limited knowledge of God, but not of a God with whom we can have fellowship. "Science may one day discover the existence on Mars of intelligent beings like men, but that scientific demonstration will not give us fellowship with them. Fellowship can be established only on the basis of mutual trust." And for knowledge of a God with whom we may have fellowship we are dependent upon revelation. "John 1:18 tells us: 'No man hath seen God at any time; the only begotten Son, which is in the bosom of the Father, he hath declared him.' And the Lord Jesus himself says, 'I am the way, and the truth, and the life; no man cometh to the Father but by me.' The truth of these two passages is borne out by the experience of countless Christians."

The Communists are inclined to charge all the evils of human life to a bad social system, as though there could be no other source for them within man himself. This,

141

Bishop Ting says, is a mistake. We cannot deny the existence of sin. "In a school where I once studied we had in the gymnasium a ball about the size of a basketball, but much heavier, and with an off-center weight in it. The result was that no matter how you tried you could not roll it straight. It was very exasperating. Is not man's life like that? In the presence of God man yesterday, today, and tomorrow still can be described in the words of Isaiah: 'All we like sheep have gone astray; we have turned every one to his own way.'"

At the same time he admits gratefully that the level of moral action has been raised under the Communist government, and says that Christians should "welcome a social system that shows itself able to raise the level of moral life. But the change of social system can only limit the effectiveness of sin, it cannot solve the problem of sin. Sin can only be healed by forgiveness, salvation, and grace."

Ting denies that in thus stressing the fact of sin he is espousing a pessimistic view of man, and points out that we are told that when the Prodigal Son repented, he "came to himself," thus evidently showing that when he was living in sin he was not himself. Man's true self is a life of righteousness, not of sin.

Then the bishop makes a direct assault upon the citadels of atheism itself. He puts forward two reasons why from the beginning of the world there have been people who would not believe in God. The first is that the moral and spiritual consequences of belief in God are greater than many people are willing to accept. He refers to the story of Adam hiding himself from God after he had sinned and says that it is natural that the man who has sinned should prefer to believe that there is no God. Even Peter knelt at Jesus' feet saying, "Lord, depart from me, for I am a sinful man." On this incident the bishop comments, "We have all had this experience of both wanting the Lord and not wanting him. The Lord is what we want, but yet he demands that we repent. If we are not willing to repent, if we are unwilling to pay the moral and spiritual price we can only ask the Lord to leave us, and even wish that he did not exist.

"Belief in God sometimes becomes an opiate, that is true. But consider how often refusal to believe in God becomes an opiate. How many men there have been since the beginning of history who have drugged themselves by a denial of God's existence, so that they could continue in sin, avoid responsibility, and stifle the reproaches of their conscience."

The second reason for the existence of atheism is that the Christian world has not let its light shine as it should. He quotes the French Catholic writer Jacques Maritain, who said that the reason why Communists espoused atheism was that the Christian world was not true to its own principles, thus arousing the hostility of Communists, who then went on from hating the Christian world to hating Christianity itself. "The sins of Christians and of the historical church have been very great, and they have brought a just punishment."

Bishop Ting concludes by pointing out that to establish the Christian church in a Communist country is a new

143

and difficult task, never before faced in the nineteen centuries of church history. "Why did the Lord give these duties to us and not to some one else? Is it because we are better? No, the Lord has his own purpose, one which we cannot fathom. But at least we know, just because our Chinese church is weak and without antecedent prestige, that we can demonstrate how the church of the Lord in weakness shows forth strength, we can show the workings of God's might, and thus give glory to God. God has indeed chosen the foolish things of the world to put to shame them that are wise, and the weak things to put to shame them that are strong. This shows that the strength is from God, and not from ourselves."

Thus ends one of the most remarkable and forthright statements that have come out of Communist China. It is a bold thing to say in a Communist country that the atheism that Communists proclaim is an opiate intended to stifle the reproaches of their own consciences.

A New Period of Suppression

The flowers of criticism that bloomed so vigorously in all levels of Chinese society in 1957, including great numbers in the Christian church, came to a sudden end in the middle of 1957. Then the period of tolerance was replaced by a new period of antirightist repression. The church was a comparatively inconspicuous part of society, and so it was not until November that the government got around to implementing its drive against rightist thought in church circles. At that time the Communists called to Peking 130

Protestant representatives from all over the country. They showed these representatives how to operate against rightists by carrying through before them the denunciations of six prominent churchmen: Liu Ling-chiu, editor of the Christian magazine *The Farmer;* Chou Ching-tse, Amoy pastor; Tung Hung-en, Shanghai pastor; Fang Ai-shih, Ningpo pastor and chairman of a Methodist church there; Chou Fu-ching, Shanghai pastor; and Marcus Cheng, veteran evangelist. These men had all been outspoken against the Communist regime during the Hundred Flowers period. Liu Ling-chiu was reported to have said that it took the Nationalist party twenty-two years to become corrupt, but that the Communist party had reached that condition in eight years. Chou Ching-tse had said that 80 per cent of the farmers were disgruntled, that the Communist officials used lies to deceive the people, that the new government was no better than the old, and that the Three Self Reform Movement was extremely detrimental to the religious life of the churches. Tung Hung-en had charged that Christians had been unjustly treated and that religious activities had been interfered with, and he had contrasted this with the true religious freedom existing in Hong Kong under British rule. Fang Ai-shih had attacked Russia for its role in the Hungarian Revolution and had even demanded that the Chinese Community party relinquish its leadership of the country. Chou Fu-ching had used his church (the Spiritual Food Church, an indigenous Chinese sect) as a forum for anticommunist heresies. Marcus Cheng had charged that the Communist party in its contemptuous

treatment of religion had committed a sin as bad as dese-
crating the tombs of one's ancestors. All of these men were
now vigorously denounced, in the same way as the denunciations of 1951 had been carried through.

The Peking delegates on their return home carried
through the same type of denunciation against churchmen
in their localities. Some local denunciations had already
taken place, notably that against Dr. Francis Wei, former
president of a Christian university in Central China, but
now the movement was intensified. Church leaders in all
parts of the country became the object of attack, if at
any time within the past two or three years they had said
anything critical of the Communist regime. In Hunan Province, where the three outstanding churches were the Church
of Christ in China, the Shun Tao Hui (of British Methodist
background) and the Lutheran Church, the leading preacher
in each of these churches was denounced and presumably
dismissed from office. In the city of Paoting, in Hopeh Province about a hundred miles south of Peking, the Congregational pastor Ma Hsing-ke was a leading figure in the
city, chairman of the Paoting City Three Self Movement,
chief of the General Affairs Department of the Paoting
Municipal First People's Hospital (probably a former mission hospital), a member of the Paoting Municipal Congress, and also of both the provincial and the city CPPCC
(Chinese People's Political Consultative Conference). He
was now charged with having opposed party and government control of religious matters. He had attacked the government Department of Religious Affairs, saying that it

was a "bureaucratic set-up" that "restricted religious activities."

It is not clear just what happened to all these church leaders who were the object of attack in this series of antirightist denunciations. One of them, the Amoy pastor Chou Ching-tse, was dismissed from his church, forbidden to preach anywhere else, and forced to earn his living by working in a factory. But the Rev. Marcus Cheng, who previously had been very active in the Three Self Movement, although denounced for having voiced criticism of the Communist party's antireligion campaign, was nevertheless able to maintain his position as a Christian leader. What happened to the other persons denounced is not a matter of public record. But since it is Communist policy not to allow anyone whom they distrust to be in a position to influence public opinion, it is likely that most of the pastors denounced lost their jobs and were put into the ranks of industrial workers. This wholesale demotion of trusted and respected church leaders all over the country must have had a very unsettling effect upon church life.

The widespread criticism of communism that was silenced by this antirightist campaign was not answered by arguments, but rather put down by repressive measures. We must suppose, therefore, that dissatisfaction with the government's religious policy still exists and is fairly widespread among Christians. If we hear less of it now than we did in 1957, that is only because it is now deprived of all opportunity to express itself.

I have spoken of those denounced as trusted and re-

147

spected church leaders. Are those who denounced them and are still prominent in the activities of the Three Self Movement equally trusted and respected, or are they looked upon by their fellow-Christians as virtual apostates? The latter is a view frequently heard in the West, and is probably also held by the Chinese friends and followers of those leaders who have been denounced. But undoubtedly a large segment of the Christian church in China accepts the leadership of the Three Self Movement and respects the men who direct it. And certainly the missionaries, who before their withdrawal from China were acquainted with Chinese leaders who later divided into these two camps, would have acknowledged the evidence of true Christian faith and loyalty both in those who later were denounced and in those who have upheld the Three Self Movement. Here then is an area where political prepossessions should not be allowed to becloud Christian judgment. A man may and should sympathize with those who have been unjustly denounced, but he must not because of this sympathy impugn the essential Christian faith of those Chinese church leaders who have honestly thought that it was their Christian duty to uphold the present government of China, or at least to work within its framework.

A Period of Radical Change

The year 1958 saw two radical programs inaugurated: the organization of communes and the Great Leap Forward in production. Of course, neither of these programs was aimed at the church, but it was inevitable that their implementation would greatly influence traditional church practice.

The organization of communes meant that the family was abandoned as the unit of production or of education. The area of private initiative in social life was now sharply curtailed. With the organization of public mess halls, of nurseries and kindergartens for the small children, and of service teams to tend to household chores, the individual Chinese found himself in a position where the return for his labor tended to be in the form of food and services rather than in the form of actual cash. The result was that from the standpoint of the individual church member the money in hand for contribution to the upkeep of his church became less and less.

Not only so, but this greater regimentation of life left the individual church member and his family with less time available for church activities. Each member of the family belonged to a different production corps, whose activities were plotted out with the precision of a military campaign —in fact the figure of a military campaign is used again and again in the description of assaults upon irrigation, harvesting, and other problems of corporate life. One result was that even the simple problem of when to hold church services—so that the majority of church members would be free to attend—became almost impossible of solution.

The Pastor and Labor

Then again, the pastor found himself in an increasingly anomalous position in a society whose every energy was being bent toward increasing material production. In all public meetings, in newspapers, and over the radio the Great Leap Forward was described and extolled as the only salvation for the country, with the corollary assumption that any one not taking an active part in it was a parasite upon society and a traitor to his country. This reasoning was not rigidly applied to schoolteachers, judges, and other white-collar workers, for their place in the scheme of things was recognized. But in a Communist society blind to the spiritual values that the pastor represents, the tendency to look upon him as a parasite and demand that he take his place in the production machine was inevitable. This attitude was so strong that one even finds in the

150

church magazine *Tien Feng* a whole series of articles denouncing the pastor's life, as heretofore lived, as a parasitic type of life, and demanding that the pastor now pull his own weight in society by contributing to economic production.

As commune organization became more complete, the exigencies of life in the smaller towns and villages enforced this demand still more. For with all of the producing sections of the populace eating in communal mess halls, even the ordinary retail distribution of food products tended to disappear from the scene, and the food moved from the fields directly to public granaries or mess hall storerooms. Supposing then that cash contributions to the pastor's support could still be maintained, where could he turn to buy food? The only way to ensure that he and his family would have food to eat was to belong to a commune, where they would be assigned to their appropriate production brigades and set to work. Today, therefore, most of the pastors in rural communities, if able to continue at all as pastors, are working full time on the farms and carrying on their pastoral duties as a spare time activity.

The same pressures have been exerted upon city pastors, though not to such an overwhelming extent. Some of them are working full time in factories. Others have banded themselves together and organized their own factories. For example, in Kweilin, capital of Kwangsi Province, Protestant ministers and Catholic priests joined together to establish the Red Light Pickle Factory in which they make soy sauce and process various kinds of pickled vegetables.

151

Since the management of this factory is in the hands of the ministers themselves, it is probable that they can adjust work schedules to allow more leeway for the requirements of pastoral work. In the reports that they have made of the finances of this factory, they have stated that the income has been sufficient to give each member of the working team a higher salary than he had had when dependent upon church members' contributions. How much time they now put in on sermon preparation and pastoral calling is not stated.

No one, not even the pastor of a large city church, is exempt from the demand that at least part of his time be spent in farm or factory work. In this demand there is no invidious singling out of pastors. All of the intellectual classes must take their turn at manual work, to an average total of perhaps two or three months out of every year. This serves a twofold purpose. On the one hand, it increases enormously the manpower available for production, and on the other, it gives every member of the intelligentsia enough taste of manual labor so that he can understand more deeply the problems and the life of the workingman. In the Communist scheme of things the workingman is supreme; not to feel at one with him is the cardinal sin. This is a laudable attitude, and one from which the free world might well learn a lesson. On the other hand, such a disregard of the sound principle of division of labor might easily result in decreased efficiency in one's own sphere of work without a corresponding gain in the other sphere, in which one still remains an outsider. Indeed, there are indications that the natural losses due to drought and floods in 1960 were increased by inept meddling in farm administration by agricultural amateurs.

For all of these reasons, therefore, the year 1958 saw a great decrease in general church activities. Congregations for the regular Sunday morning church service fell off alarmingly. The city of Peking began 1958 with sixty-five churches, many of them originally with substantial membership. (Before his arrest Wang Ming-tao had regularly preached to congregations of more than a thousand every Sunday.) But by the middle of the year, a Christian reporter in Peking could say that there were not more than five hundred in attendance at church in all these churches of Peking on a Sunday morning. The same situation was reported from all the cities in China.

Church Unification

The result of the decline in membership was to increase enormously the demand for the consolidation of all Protestant activities. Just as churches of different denominations in America will hold union meetings during July and August when their attendance falls off because of the "summer slump," so the demand arose for union meetings in all cities where more than one denomination was at work. In Peking, out of all those sixty-five churches, four were chosen to remain open, one each in the north, south, east, and west sections of the city. The other churches were all closed, and, as a patriotic gesture, this now unused property was turned over to the government for public use. A large number of preachers, Bible women, and theological students were released by this step for participation in the Great Leap Forward, and we are told that 150 from Peking were assigned to labor in a farm commune.

Shanghai had formerly had over two hundred churches. These were now reduced in number to twenty-three. In the city of Soochow only one church remained open, though later it was found necessary to reopen another.

It seems clear that the reason for this wholesale merger of Protestant activities in the summer of 1958 was the very practical one indicated above. However, the revolt against the denominationalism imported from the West was also a contributing factor. For this revolt it must be said that the missions themselves had laid the groundwork. For years the pastors of the various denominations in China had been trained in union theological seminaries and most of the great Christian universities of the country were run on a union basis. There were also other institutions, such as hospitals and some middle schools, that were joint projects of more than one denomination. Moreover, even in the mother countries the reason for existence of many of the separate denominations has largely lost its edge—they preach practically the same gospel, and differ only in comparatively insignificant details of church organization and practice. Indeed, the separateness of these denominations is often maintained only by appeal to the vested interests involved. It will not seem surprising, therefore, that the Chinese church in the past has suffered these denominational distinctions only out of polite deference to the missionaries and mission boards, and that now, with those influences withdrawn, the churches should inevitably gravitate toward a closer union with each other.

It is to be noted that so far there has been no real merger of the churches, but only a worshiping together. But a worshiping together that is to continue all the year round, and that involves the liquidation of the former separate church properties, is a very different thing from the summer slump union services that we are familiar with in America. There is no ultimate end of fusing the separate corporate existences in the latter program. The Chinese Christians, on the other hand, are plainly saying that the delay in official merger is only for the purpose of getting better acquainted with each other before entering on the negotiations that will make one organized Protestant church of the multifarious denominations hitherto existing in China.

The Three Self Reform Movement, which by this time had an organized headquarters in every province and in every major city, and which was recognized by the Religious Affairs Bureau of the People's Republic as the spokesman for Protestant Christianity, was the agency through which all the necessary actions for unifying the church program took place. Each city took its own action, and there was apparently no need felt to refer any of this action to corresponding denominational authorities for confirmation. The details of union varied from place to place, but a typical example is the city of Taiyuan, capital of Shansi Province. This large city had churches of the following denominations: Church of Christ in China, Brethren, Assemblies of God, China Inland Mission, Seventh-day Adventist, Salvation Army, and the indigenous Little Flock. In addition there was a Taiyuan Y.M.C.A. Here are the articles of union, as agreed upon by all these organizations:

There shall be unified worship for the city of Taiyuan, and a ministerial staff of three or four. All fellow workers besides these, and those assigned to the Three Self office, shall throw themselves into the socialist construction of our mother country. Those who are older or physically weak shall retire. All real and movable church property and all church funds shall be turned over to the Three Self Committee.

CHURCH ORGANIZATION

1. All former governing committees and boards of the various churches are hereby abolished, and the administration of the church shall be in the hands of the Three Self Committee.
2. Regarding ritual, regulations, and church order:
   a. There shall be a unified worship program, and each church shall surrender its own individual ritual.
   b. The hymns used in worship shall be unified, and a committee shall choose and edit the hymns for use.
   c. All books used in the interpretation of the Bible shall be examined and judged, and those containing poisonous thoughts shall be rejected. Only teachings favoring union and socialism shall be used. In particular, any material coming from outside [probably referring to material sent in by mail from Hong Kong] shall be carefully examined before being accepted.
   d. There shall be no more teaching about the Last Day, or about the vanity of this world. This is negative and pessimistic teaching. Instead we shall emphasize the

need for the union of faith and practice, the dignity of labor, the control of nature, and the dividing line between ourselves and our enemies, between right and wrong.

    e. Belief and unbelief shall not be made an issue in determining marriage questions.

3. In regard to the necessary reform of each church:

    a. The Little Flock shall abolish its women's meetings, its weekly breaking of bread, its personal interviews with members before the breaking of bread, and its rule against women speaking in the church.

    b. The Salvation Army shall give up all its military regulations.

    c. The Seventh-day Adventists shall abolish their daily morning prayers. On the Sabbath they shall participate in beneficial good works and in economic production. Their tithe system for the support of the clergy shall be abolished, and also their unification of accounts for Shansi Province.

    d. All the Y.M.C.A. secretaries shall be assigned to productive labor, and the closing of the Taiyuan Y.M.C.A. as a separate organization shall be carefully considered.

It will be seen from the above that even those sects that in Western experience have shown themselves most uncooperative with the main body of Protestant Christianity are an integral part of this unification plan. Not only the Seventh-day Adventists referred to above, but also the Southern Baptists, various Pentecostal sects, and ultraconservative bodies that in the West refuse to take part in any ecumenical movements have apparently all shelved, at least for the time being, their distinctive tenets in order to merge themselves in this unification movement.

It may be thought that this acquiescence was due to heavy political pressure that the Christian leaders concerned did not dare oppose. This is possibly true, but if so the pressure was hidden and indirectly applied. The head of the Religious Affairs Bureau has denied any interference, and this denial has been confirmed by individual Christian leaders. When the Rev. Chao Fu-san of the Sheng Kung Hui (Anglican) visited Australia in November, 1959, he was asked if the adoption of unified worship was due to government compulsion. To this he replied, "Not at all. To my knowledge no one has ever suggested that the government interferes in any way in matters of church order. There has been some movement toward unity from the top, as it were. But the main impetus has come from the congregations themselves, all over China."

Further confirmation of the voluntary nature of this unification comes from Miss Liao Hung-yin, a Chinese Christian who was formerly professor of chemistry in the mission-established West China Union University. In 1944 she married a member of the British Embassy and went to London to live. In 1959 she revisited China and had an opportunity to talk with old friends in Chengtu. Here one of the denominations involved in the merger was a Quaker church, established by a British Friends mission. In talking with several of her Quaker friends she learned that after sitting together with the other denominations for several months they had decided that they didn't feel at home in that kind of service and would go back to their own meeting for worship. She added that other denominations were talking of doing the same. It seems clear from this report that the decision whether to merge or not is entirely in the hands of the Christians themselves. Apparently by the fall of 1959, there had been some reaction against the initial enthusiasm for unification in the city of Chengtu, but there has been no indication in the news from other places of any turning back in the plans for ultimate unification of all Protestantism.

On the whole it would seem that Chinese Christians have not as a rule been convinced by their missionary instructors that the points of doctrine and church rule that divide Christians are of any major concern. Those who have followed the progress of church union movements in other places, notably in South India and in North India, are aware that the chief point of difficulty is the adjustment of episcopal and non-episcopal doctrines of church organization. The Anglican family of churches holds that all ordained ministers must have been ordained by a bishop in the apostolic succession. This has always been the most controversial of the four points contained in the Lambeth Quadrilateral, adopted by the Lambeth Conference in 1888 as a four-point basis for the reunion of Christendom. (The other three are the sufficiency of the Scriptures as the standard of faith; adherence to the Apostles' and Nicene Creeds; and acceptance of the two sacraments of baptism and the Lord's Supper.) The Rev. Chao Fu-san commented on this point when he was in Australia in 1959. When asked if the question of ministerial orders would not be an insuperable obstacle to organic union, he replied, "You must not say insuperable. It is a matter of our Lord's will. At the present moment, it is something that has still to be discussed. You know that the Sheng Kung Hui stands firmly on the Lambeth Quadrilateral. I do feel that the majority of our bishops enjoy a weighty prestige among all Christians in China. I think this will count, perhaps more than in South India."

It is to be presumed, therefore, that some of the more creative minds among Chinese Christian leaders are already engaged in exploring the lines along which the organic union of all Protestant Christianity in China may take place. Their strategy of worshiping together for several years before attempting to work out the terms of union is undoubtedly a wise one. For in that process, the nontheological psychological barriers that so often separate Christians of different sects will be gradually broken down. As a result, when Chinese Christians do decide to sit down around a conference table for serious discussion of the terms of union, there probably will be much more of the irenic spirit of give and take than there otherwise would be.

In spite of the advantages of union, the diminishing scale of church activities that has led to this unification movement is an ominous sign. It is true that Christians can remain true to their faith even when they do not have an opportunity to worship together, but it is also true that the average Christian needs the stimulus of corporate worship, and any social system that lessens appreciably the possibility of such meetings, as we find it in the fanatic devotion to the Great Leap Forward in industrial production, is to be deplored. On the other hand, the creative and resourceful spirit in which Chinese Christian leaders have met this challenge, using it to bring about a deeper unity in Christian witness, is a hopeful sign. It indicates that loyalty to the Master will not easily be eradicated from the minds and hearts of Christians in China.

Today and Tomorrow

From the preceding account it is apparent that something of a modus vivendi has been arrived at between Protestant Christianity and the Chinese Communist party. The latter, so far, is willing to recognize the former and guarantees a certain degree of freedom of religious belief, on the condition that Chinese Christians show themselves loyal citizens and co-operate in the establishment of a new economic order.

These conditions of acceptance and co-operation are not in themselves necessarily subversive of the principles of Christian liberty. Throughout the two thousand years of church history, many a Christian has exhibited loyalty to a government no more deserving of it than the People's Republic of China and has worked through and supported a variety of economic systems. It is therefore understandable that most Christian leaders in China have accepted these conditions, and that the Christian church has in consequence received government recognition and been accorded a modest niche in Chinese society, so that it has not been compelled to go underground.

This does not mean that the future position of the Christian church is assured. The Chinese Communist party remains as blatantly atheistic as ever, and if the pressures exerted upon the small Christian community succeed in undermining its will to continue its witness to the gospel, the party can be counted on to administer in due time the *coup de grâce*. What then, as we look at the situation in China today, are the prospects for the future?

There are a number of grounds for deep concern. In the first place, many of the most courageous and creative voices in Chinese Christianity have been silenced. Methodist Bishop W. Y. Ch'en, Sheng Kung Hui Bishops Kimber Den and Stephen Chang, independent evangelist Wang Ming-tao, the deeply consecrated and creative leaders of the True Jesus Church, the Little Flock, and the Jesus Family, and many influential pastors in all denominations have been imprisoned or dismissed from their churches and forbidden to preach. This persecution has greatly impoverished the church, although that does not of itself nullify the terms of the modus vivendi referred to above. For in every case the ostensible ground for action against any Christian leader imprisoned or dismissed was political and nonreligious. On the other hand, the large number that were silenced gives ground for suspicion that the government was not at all averse to silencing any Christian leader against whom an excuse of subversive or reactionary activity could be plausibly trumped up. This suspicion is

163

deepened when one reads the denunciatory articles and finds an astonishingly flimsy web of factual evidence adduced against most of them.

There is further ground for concern in the "bamboo curtain" drawn between the Chinese Christian church and the Protestant Christianity of the West with which it was formerly so closely allied. The departure of the missionaries and the cutting off of mission funds was not necessarily a calamity, for this development gave more scope for true Chinese leadership. But the refusal (or inability) to take part in meetings of the World Council of Churches and the cutting of all ties with sister denominations in the West is a very unfortunate restriction in Christian fellowship. Chinese Christians feel keenly the resulting isolation and frequently voice a hope for the ultimate re-establishment of friendly relations. But the political web in which they are caught up makes it necessary for them to keep repeating the charge that the Western church is the tool of imperialism. As a matter of fact Western churches as a whole are much freer of governmental control than the Chinese church is, and not infrequently pronounce judgment upon unchristian acts of their own governments, something which almost none of the present Chinese Christian leaders have yet ventured to do. But the involvement of churches on both sides in the political and social views of their own governments will make the renewal of friendly church contacts impossible for a long time to come.

Again, there has been a shocking diminution in concrete church activities as a result of the Communist policy in

China. Regular church services, Bible study classes, Sunday schools, prayer meetings, women's meetings, though all legal and permitted, have steadily decreased in number and scope as life has become more and more regimented in a program that leaves no time for the things of the Spirit. Church publications have also decreased almost to the vanishing point. Few serious books of theology or Bible study have appeared since the Communists came to power; the only ones advertised in *Tien Feng* have been fundamentalist leader Chia Yü-ming's *Bible Notes* and Nanking Seminary's version of the *Little Flowers of St. Francis*. Christian periodicals have one by one dropped off until for a number of years the only survivor on a national scale has been *Tien Feng*, first a weekly and now a monthly magazine, published in Shanghai and serving the whole of Protestant Christianity. Finally the number of theological schools serving the church has greatly decreased, and the number of students now being trained for the ministry, probably a total for the whole country of not more than 250, is pitifully inadequate for the needs of a church of 700,000 members, not to speak of the lack of hope for an aggressive evangelistic program that can bring a steady increase in membership and strength.

This decrease of outward activities would not be so alarming if one could feel assured that what does continue is a true and faithful witness to Christian truth. But, as already noted, there is evidence that the pressure of Communist propaganda has caused a watering down and in some cases even a perversion of Christian teaching. One

Lutheran pastor, well trained in the best seminaries of the West, could yet say that the Christian teaching that all men are sinners is too pessimistic, that most folks are pretty good, and it is only landlords, capitalists, and exploiters that are bad. Such doctrines as those of the Second Coming and of the Final Judgment do not fit in with Communist dogma, and so Christian preachers are warned not to preach on such themes. The Bible is still there, to keep calling Chinese Christians back to the pure gospel, but it is increasingly being reinterpreted in such a way as not to conflict with Communist doctrines.

In the field of ethical conduct, too, there have been backward steps. Christian spokesmen for the present regime are accustomed to claim that the moral level has been greatly raised in the systematic care for the sick and the needy, and the increasing dignity of life of those formerly despised. To the extent that this is true—and it is a very considerable extent—we may return profound thanks to God, and may even believe that in the long run this positive achievement will overbalance the losses that have been experienced in other lines. But it must be said that the influence of Communist propaganda upon the Christian church has caused it to fall into two grave faults: a lessened regard for the truth, and an acquiescence in hate campaigns.

As one reads the denunciatory articles that have filled Christian periodicals in China since 1951, it becomes apparent that many of the charges leveled against the Western church, the mission boards, the missionaries, and many of their own Chinese colleagues have little if any

166

basis in fact. In the desire to substantiate the charge that the whole mission movement was the tool of imperialism, perfectly innocent actions have been twisted and given sinister interpretations. For example, any maps of China or of local areas in China that were found in the library or among the papers of any missionary were put forward as evidence that he was engaged in spying activity, even though they were ordinary maps sold in any bookstore.

Again, the expressions of hatred that have filled the pages of Christian magazines in China since 1951 are an appalling indication of a church subservient to the Communist line. Men who had been honored and respected members of the Christian community are now denounced by their friends with coarse epithets and in highly unchristian terms of virulent hatred. It is true that their Christian conscience was uneasy at participating in this campaign of hatred, and so we find a whole series of articles in the *Tien Feng* trying to prove that Jesus' command to love our enemies does not really mean what it says, and that these virulent expressions are no more than what Jesus himself used against the Pharisees. But it is hard to see how a church that gives itself over so completely to feelings of partisan hatred can be an effective witness to the Christian gospel.

Finally, the surviving church in China is steadily exposed to the eroding effect of an all-powerful government that openly and systematically scoffs at all religion as superstition and discriminates against Christians, if not officially at least unofficially, in many of its actions. When bright high school graduates are refused permission to go to college because as Christians they are considered "politically unreliable," when Christian doctors, nurses, and teachers find it harder to obtain recognition and promotion than their non-Christian colleagues, it takes a strong Christian faith to endure such discrimination with patience. It is not surprising then that so many whose faith was not strong enough have quietly dropped all claim to being Christians.

This is a saddening picture, and it is not to be wondered at that some in the West have concluded that true Christian faith no longer exists in China except in scattered individuals and in certain hidden and underground activities. These critics feel that the leaders of the Three Self Reform Movement, who claim to represent a continuing church in China, are not really worthy of the name and should not be so recognized. But those who make this charge fail to consider that if these Three Self leaders had really abandoned their Christian faith, their easiest course of procedure would be just to drop out of the Christian church altogether. The fact that they remain in the church, and accept the obloquy that this connection entails, is a proof that the Christian message has entered deeply into their souls. If they do not make a perfect application of it in their own lives, then let him who is without offense in this regard cast the first stone.

And so the very fact that the church still exists after these years of Communist domination and propaganda is something of a hopeful sign. Though the number of professing Christians is not as large as it was in 1949, their fundamental allegiance to Christ must be deep and strong, or they would not now be in the church at all.

Still more, the church is continuing to bear witness to the gospel in such a way as to bring about conversions and baptisms. As long as there was any concrete church news in *Tien Feng* at all, baptisms continued to be reported, and a significant number of them were on confession of faith, and not just the baptism of children in Christian families. Church news practically disappeared from *Tien Feng* after the unification of worship in the summer and fall of 1958, but that does not mean that the church's witness to the gospel came to a standstill. A private letter from Soochow states that in the 1959 Christmas service more than thirty persons were baptized.

Chinese church leaders, too, seem confident that the church in China will not only continue a bare existence, but will advance. As late as January 1961, after all the pressures that we have described had had their effect upon organized Christianity in China, 319 delegates from all parts of China attended a nationwide conference of the Three Self Reform Movement held in Shanghai, and a forty-nine-member standing committee was elected to direct the future course of the movement. When it is remembered that this movement to all intents and purposes now represents the Protestant church in China, it is apparent that its leaders are not thinking in terms of an early demise of the Chinese church.

It must be remembered, too, that the "bamboo curtain" is not as impenetrable as it may seem to the American observer. It is true that Americans cannot travel freely in China, but this restriction does not apply to Christians from other countries, and Christian visitors from both Communist and non-Communist countries have continued to visit the church in China. This fact is bound to have a steadying effect on any possible waverers in the Christian ranks there.

Thus in casting up a balance of the unfavorable and the favorable factors at work in the Chinese church, it is evident that though the situation may give ground for deep concern, it is not hopeless, and the Chinese church must not be written off as either nonexistent or apostate. No one can know what the next ten years will see: The church, already shorn of much of its outward standing, may quietly disappear as an organized force in Chinese society, or it may go on to a renewed vigor and witness. The Western church, which through its missionary work has been so closely bound up with the development of this church in the past, is now largely helpless. It can do little more than pray that Christians in China remain true to the gospel that they have received. This we can and should do, at the same time praying that we in the West do nothing in our individual or corporate life that would throw a stumbling block in the way of our Chinese brethren. Rather may we so act as to hasten a renewal of that fellowship that Christ intended when he prayed that his followers might be one.

SUGGESTIONS FOR FURTHER READING

BACKGROUND ON CHINA

Goodrich, Luther Carrington. *Short History of the Chinese People* (3rd ed.). New York: Harper & Brothers, 1959. One of the best of the shorter histories.

Latourette, Kenneth Scott. *The Chinese, Their History and Culture* (3rd. ed. rev.). New York: The Macmillan Co., 1946. A comprehensive survey by an eminent historian and former missionary in China.

Rowe, David Nelson. *Modern China: A Brief History* (Anvil paperback). New York: Van Nostrand Co., Inc., 1959. About evenly divided between a history of the past 120 years and source readings covering the same period.

Stuart, John Leighton. *Fifty Years in China.* . . . New York: Random House, Inc., 1954. Autobiography of an eminent Presbyterian missionary (Presb. U.S.), former president of Yenching University in Peking, and the last American ambassador to China.

Varg, Paul A. *Missionaries, Chinese, and Diplomats: the American Protestant Missionary Movement in China, 1890-1952.* Princeton, N. J.: Princeton Univ. Press, 1958. A reading of this book will show how it is possible for the Communists to charge the missionary enterprise with being an agent of imperialism.

BACKGROUND ON COMMUNISM

Bennett, John Coleman. *Christianity and Communism Today* (rev. ed.). New York: Association Press, 1960. The author's purpose is to show what Christianity can learn from communism, and on the other hand to bring the insights of the Christian faith to bear on an appraisal of the Communist philosophy.

Hunt, Robert Nigel Carew. *Theory and Practice of Communism; An Introduction* (rev. ed.). New York: The Macmillan Co., 1951. A well balanced survey of European communism from Marx to Stalin.

West, Charles Converse. *Communism and the Theologians: A Study of an Encounter.* Philadelphia: Westminster Press, 1958. How five representative theologians of today (Tillich, Berdyaev, Niebuhr, Barth, and Hromadka) regard communism. This study is of special interest because Hromadka, who lives in Czechoslovakia, gives a favorable interpretation of communism and thus helps readers to understand how Chinese Christian leaders today can follow that line.

HISTORY OF CHRISTIAN MISSIONS IN CHINA

Bates, M. Searle. *The Protestant Enterprise in China, 1900-1950* (working title). This is a book-in-progress that is scheduled for publication possibly late in 1962 or early in 1963. The book will emphasize the Chinese church more than foreign missions and can be recommended heartily.

Cary-Elwes, Columba. *China and the Cross; A Survey of Missionary History.* New York: P. J. Kenedy & Son, 1957. A history of Roman Catholic missions and the Catholic Church in China. An excellent history, and always fair and friendly in the occasional references to Protestant work.

Latourette, Kenneth Scott. *History of Christian Missions in China*. New York: The Macmillan Co., 1929. This is the standard work on the subject and includes both Protestant and Roman Catholic mission developments up to the 1920's.

COMMUNISM IN CHINA

Barnett, A. Doak. *Communist China and Asia: Challenge to American Policy* (published for the American Council on Foreign Relations). New York: Harper & Brothers, 1960. Barnett was born in China, the son of a Y.M.C.A. secretary, and is now Associate Professor of Government, Columbia University. In this book he shows how all the uncommitted countries of Asia are watching China and comparing her with India to see which system is more effective in bringing about economic growth.

Ch'en, Hsi-en. *Thought Reform of the Chinese Intellectuals*. New York: Oxford University Press, 1960. An outstanding Chinese scholar, now on the faculty of the University of Southern California, describes brain-washing from a less emotional standpoint than Edward Hunter, but with equally scathing conclusions.

Durdin, Peggy. *Mao's China* (Headline series, no. 136). New York: Foreign Policy Association, 1959. A popular account. Author is the daughter of China missionary parents and she herself taught in Shanghai American School. She is now resident in Hong Kong, the wife of a New York Times China correspondent.

Faure, Edgar. *The Serpent and the Tortoise; Problems of the New China*. Translated by Lovett F. Edwards. New York: St. Martins Press, Inc., 1958. A former French premier tells of his visit to China in 1956, throwing particular light on the Hundred Flowers period and its aftermath.

Hunter, Edward. *Brain-Washing in Red China; the Calculated Destruction of Men's Minds* (new and enlarged ed.). New York: The Vanguard Press, 1953. An exposure of the pressures used in thought reform, written from the standpoint of a dedicated anticommunist.

Rickett, Allyn and Adele. *Prisoners of Liberation*. New York: Cameron Associates, Inc., 1957. An autobiographical account of the experiences of two Fulbright scholars in Peking, who spent five years in a Communist prison, underwent the rigors of brain-washing, and came out convinced that the process had given them a new social conscience.

Schwartz, Benjamin Isadore. *Chinese Communism and the Rise of Mao* (Russian Research Studies, no. 4). Cambridge, Mass.: Harvard Univ. Press, 1951. A scholarly analysis of the Chinese Communist party, stressing particularly its early history.

Seligman, Eustace and Walker, Richard L. *Should the United States Change Its China Policy?* (Headline series, no. 129). New York: Foreign Policy Association, 1958. Summation of views pro and con for a change in U. S. policy, with Seligman answering "yes" and Walker "no."

Walker, Richard Louis. *China Under Communism: the First Five Years*. New Haven, Conn.: Yale Univ. Press, 1956. An objective description.

THE CHURCHES UNDER COMMUNISM

China Bulletin, edited by Francis P. Jones for the National Council of Churches, Division of Foreign Missions, Far Eastern Office, 475 Riverside Drive, New York 28, New York. Published bi-weekly from 1952 to April 1961, and monthly since that time. Complete file through 1958 available on microfilm. The news in the *Bulletin* is spotty and fragmentary, and often hard to interpret, but it represents the only attempt to supply the West with continuous news of the Chinese churches during this critical period.

SUGGESTIONS FOR FURTHER READING

China Consultation 1958 and *China Consultation 1960*. New York: National Council of Churches, Division of Foreign Missions, Far Eastern Office, 1958; 1960. Two pamphlets giving reports of conferences held under the auspices of the China Committee of the Far Eastern Office.

Hunter, Edward. *The Story of Mary Liu*. London, Eng.: Hodder & Stoughton, Ltd., 1956. A vivid and frightening account of the "denunciation meetings" that were held all over China to "reform" the thinking of the people.

James, Alfred Francis. *Reports of Deputation of Australian Churchmen to Mainland China*. New York: National Council of Churches, Division of Foreign Missions, Far Eastern Office, 1957. Mr. James was a member of the Australian Anglican team that visited China in 1956. This report of the trip is reprinted from the *Episcopal Churchnews*.

Lyall, Leslie T. *Come Wind, Come Weather; the Present Experience of the Church in China*. Chicago: The Moody Press, 1960. A somber account of what has happened to the churches of China under communism, with somewhat severe conclusions.

Martinson, Harold. *Red Dragon Over China*. Minneapolis, Minn.: Augsburg Publishing House, 1956. Author is more concerned over what happened to the missionaries than with what happened to the Chinese churches.

Outerbridge, Leonard Mallory. *The Lost Churches of China*. Philadelphia: Westminster Press, 1952. A rather pessimistic presentation.

Stockwell, Francis Olin. *With God in Red China; the Story of Two Years in Chinese Communist Prisons*. New York: Harper & Brothers, 1953. An account by a Methodist missionary of his experiences.

Quakers Visit China. London, Eng.: The Society of Friends East-West Relations Committee and Peace Committee, n.d.

175

SUGGESTIONS FOR FURTHER READING

A very readable and well-balanced account of the visit of six British Quakers to China in 1955.

THEORY AND PRACTICE OF MISSIONS

Allen, Roland. *The Ministry of the Spirit: Selected Writings . . . ,* ed. David Paton. London, Eng.: World Dominion Press, 1960.

Christian Witness in Communist China, Brother Barnabas, pseud. New York: Morehouse-Gorham Co., Inc., 1951.

Hayward, Victor E. W. *Ears to Hear.* London, Eng.: Edinburgh House Press, 1955.

Paton, David Macdonald. *Christian Missions and the Judgement of God.* Napierville, Ill.: A. E. Allenson, Inc., 1953.

Index

177

INDEX

INDEX

A NOTE ABOUT THE FORMAT

The text of this book is set in Linotype Caledonia,
10 point leaded 3 points. Designed by the
late W. A. Dwiggins, this face belongs to the "modern"
family of type faces and is somewhat similar
to Scotch Modern, although more freely drawn than
that letter.

Manufactured by Sowers Printing Company, Lebanon, Pa.
Jackets and paper covers by Affiliated Lithographers, Inc.,
    New York
Map by Rafael Palacios
Paper: S. D. Warren's #66 Antique
Typographic design by Margery W. Smith
Binding design by Louise E. Jefferson